FORMING TRUE
Partnerships

How AA members use the
program to improve relationships

Stories from AA Grapevine

BOOKS PUBLISHED BY AA GRAPEVINE, INC.

The Language of the Heart (& eBook)
The Best of the Grapevine Volume I (& eBook)
The Best of Bill (& eBook)
Thank You for Sharing
Spiritual Awakenings (& eBook)
I Am Responsible: The Hand of AA
The Home Group: Heartbeat of AA (& eBook)
Emotional Sobriety — The Next Frontier (& eBook)
Spiritual Awakenings II (& eBook)
In Our Own Words: Stories of Young AAs in Recovery (& eBook)
Beginners' Book (& eBook)
Voices of Long-Term Sobriety (& eBook)
A Rabbit Walks Into A Bar
Step by Step — Real AAs, Real Recovery (& eBook)
Emotional Sobriety II — The Next Frontier (& eBook)
Young & Sober (& eBook)
Into Action (& eBook)
Happy, Joyous & Free (& eBook)
One on One (& eBook)
No Matter What (& eBook)
Grapevine Daily Quote Book (& eBook)
Sober & Out (& eBook)
Forming True Partnerships (& eBook)
Our Twelve Traditions (& eBook)
Making Amends (& eBook)
Voices of Women in AA (& eBook)

IN SPANISH

El lenguaje del corazón
Lo mejor de Bill (& eBook)
El grupo base: Corazón de AA
Lo mejor de La Viña
Felices, alegres y libres (& eBook)
Un día a la vez (& eBook)

IN FRENCH

Le langage du coeur
Les meilleurs articles de Bill
Le Groupe d'attache: Le battement du coeur des AA
En tête à tête (& eBook)
Heureux, joyeux et libres (& eBook)

FORMING TRUE
Partnerships

How AA members use the program to improve relationships

Stories from AA Grapevine

AAGRAPEVINE,Inc.

New York, New York

WWW. AAGRAPEVINE.ORG

AA PREAMBLE

Alcoholics Anonymous is a fellowship of people
who share their experience, strength and hope
with each other that they may solve their common problem
and help others to recover from alcoholism.

The only requirement for membership is a desire to stop drinking.
There are no dues or fees for AA membership;
we are self-supporting through our own contributions.
AA is not allied with any sect, denomination, politics, organization
or institution; does not wish to engage in any controversy,
neither endorses nor opposes any causes.

Our primary purpose is to stay sober
and help other alcoholics to achieve sobriety.

©AA Grapevine, Inc.

Contents

AA Preamble .... *V*
Welcome .... *XIII*

CHAPTER ONE

The Family

Where both alcoholism and the joys of recovery hit home

A Family Affair *August 2010*.................................... 2
A Box of Pears *September 2014*.................................. 7
My Father's AA *March 2005*.................................... 10
I Stole the Wallet *August 2010*.................................. 16
Cartoons and Bourbon *March 2014*............................ 18
Letting Go in Florida *March 2014* 20
Struck Sober *August 2010* 24
Game Changer *December 2010*.................................. 25
How My Child Came to Believe *August 1962*.................... 29
Oil and Water *April 2007* 31
A Letter Every Week *December 2014* 34

CHAPTER TWO

Marriage and Divorce

We don't have to drink over love, or the loss of it

Are AA Marriages Different? *January 1983* 38

Marriage—Drunk and Sober *February 2003* 39

A Love Story *May 1998* 42

Sobriety and Divorce *October 1977* 48

Marriage *March 1980* 50

Just Friends *May 2010* 51

Let's Get a Divorce! *January 1977* 55

Love Story *November 1958* 58

Finding Love Again on AA Campus *March 2011* 61

A Square *April 1960* 65

CHAPTER THREE

Dating and Romance

Getting out there and navigating the dating game
without a glass in hand

Relationships Reconsidered *November 2013* 72

Happily Together in Recovery *February 2003* 75

Looking for Love *March 1984* 76

Hey There, Lonely Guy *February 2008* 78

With or Without Him *February 2008* 81

Prime Dating Material? *February 2008* 85

Me and You and AA *November 2013* 88

Letting Go of the Golden Glow *April 2014* 90

Saturday Night *May 2008* 93

A 14-Year-Old Mind in a 35-Year-Old Body *May 1999* 98

CHAPTER FOUR

On the Job

Learning to become a worker among workers

It Works at Work *June 2000* 104

I Almost Lost My Job—Sober *August 1984* 106

Serenity Chair *May 2001* 108

The Misfit *May 2011* *109*

Putting Up With Mr. Bill *January 2003* *111*

Planting the Seed *February 2010* *113*

The Program at Work *January 2012* *114*

It Works at Work (If You Work It) *December 2000* *116*

Payback Time *April 2007* *119*

CHAPTER FIVE

Friendship

*Satisfying, lasting relationships are counted among the
Fellowship's great gifts*

A Circle of Friends *December 1992* *124*

Where Everybody Knows My Name *October 2010* *125*

Listening to Walter *August 2010.* *129*

Garage Opener *March 2009* *130*

The Cheetah and His Bubba *June 2000* *133*

More Fun Than TV *August 2003* *136*

Friends for Life *January 1993* *137*

Winning Friends *March 2002* *141*

Best Friends *December 2011* *143*

Real Friends *May 2011* *146*

CHAPTER SIX

Pets and Animals

*Sometimes victims of our addiction, they become
one of recovery's rewards*

A Canine Step Nine *March 2013.* *150*

Ala-Cat *September 1983.* *151*

Puppy Love *February 2003* *154*

Jake *February 1984.* *156*

A Fox in the Woods *October 2001* *158*

For the Love of Ruby *March 2002* *159*

A Friendly Dog Story *July 2003* *162*

Tiger in the Tank *April 2009* *163*

CHAPTER SEVEN

Sponsorship

Experience, guidance, love and sobriety are the gifts of this special one-on-one bond

Sponsor Relationships *September 1975* *166*

90 Days of June *February 2015* *169*

Dumped *February 2012* *172*

An Unfamiliar Bond *March 2008*. *175*

Quiet Guidance *May 1990* *180*

The Choice *June 1991* *186*

... And Learn *November 1996* *188*

Sweet Goodbye at the Farm *January 2013* *189*

A Kid Like Me *March 2009* *191*

Words of Love *June 1991* *194*

Under the Renoir *February 2015* *195*

Twelve Steps *198*

Twelve Traditions. *199*

About AA and AA Grapevine. *200*

WELCOME

"Having thus cleaned away the debris of the past, we consider how, with our newfound knowledge of ourselves, we may develop the best possible relations with every human being we know."
—Step Eight, *Twelve Steps and Twelve Traditions*

Relationships are where we turn for life support. A life-giving partnership with anyone or anything requires the engagement of a whole self, exactly what active alcoholics lack—and what they are seeking in the bottle. The stories in this book, written by the readers of AA Grapevine, illustrate why the ability to enjoy healthy relationships of every kind is one of the most challenging goals of recovery, and one of its most prized gifts.

The seven chapters here honor the many different categories of relationships our members seek to heal, beginning with a section on families. When we get sober and get the family right, the great shift toward sanity begins; then getting picked on is less likely to mean picking up a drink. It's then we realize, writes the author of "How My Child Came to Believe," that "time, if we but give it, will not only restore but sanctify."

Marriage, that pressure cooker, can be the breeding ground for chaos or the birthplace of recovery, as we see in the chapter on marriage. These stunningly candid stories take us through marital adventures and sober divorces, illuminating many facets of that volatile institution and offering fresh new uses for the Serenity Prayer.

In the chapter on dating and romance, one writer seeks love under the spell of alcohol's "weird mental-emotional spin." In the story "A 14-Year-Old Mind in a 35-Year-Old Body," he describes the brand of dating we sometimes refer to as "hostage-taking." In "Relationships Reconsidered," Jeff H. paints a different picture. "By continuing to trust God and clean house," he writes, "this relationship is completely effortless!"

"AA can bring people together, no matter what their differences," says April A. in "Planting the Seed." Really? Even our co-workers? The stories in the chapter on the workplace say yes. Workplaces are trying, but when we acknowledge sobriety as our primary full-time job, the Promises come true. Friendship, feared and longed for by alcoholic loners, is prized by AA members. In "Winning Friends," T.T. puts it this way: "I entered AA as a lonely, wretched, ignorant and isolated practicing drunk, and I found what I always wanted—to be part of something wonderful and to be valued by others."

Our four-legged friends are important figures in so many of our addiction and recovery stories. The particularly poignant chapter on pets and animals reminds us that our most forgiving animal companions are likely to act as our mirrors, that a living amends can be a Frisbee toss or a clean litter box, and that some of our best button-pushers have nine lives.

And in the book's final chapter, we see wonderful examples of how the two-way relationship of AA sponsor and sponsee may be like no other in the world. The author of "90 Days of June," Carol P., writes as a grateful newcomer: "For a long time I was out of sight of the herd, and now I've been accepted into the fold. All this in 90 days, all because I was willing to reach out for help to a sponsor."

We are "part of a great whole," says Tradition One. No matter what version of a relationship an alcoholic is dealing with, sobriety is capable of healing it, stabilizing it, and ensuring its longevity. The stories in *Forming True Partnerships* show that by putting the drink down and getting involved in the AA program, we get the chance to heal old relationships and develop wonderful, new, healthy ones. That's quite a considerable gift.

CHAPTER ONE

The Family

Where both alcoholism and the joys of recovery hit home

Alcoholism has always been a family business. As the stories in this section on the family happily illustrate, so is sobriety. Our writers in this chapter reinforce the truths we live by in fresh, insightful ways. "One by one we crashed into the rooms of AA," writes Kirk K. in "Struck Sober," yet "the disease lives on even as we try to break the chain in our generation."

These accounts of recovery's ripple effects through families once shredded by active alcoholism offer their own kind of quiet drama. In "A Family Affair," Alan D. reports the birth of the first child on either side of his family to be born to sober parents. H.W., in the story "How My Child Came to Believe," describes herself, a sobering parent, as one "who has returned to the human community through the healing influence of the AA life," and is grateful for her attorney, also in recovery, who offers her a profound, unique take on regaining custody and "spiritual rights."

In "Game Changer," Susan B. gets caught up in comparing her alcoholic dad to the father in "The Brady Bunch" and, after she finally gets to her first meeting, her father greets his birthday with a message to her: "You never have to give me another birthday present for the rest of my life."

A Family Affair
August 2010

This is the story of my family and what AA has done for us. This is a sober story. Suffice it to say we all belong. It starts with my father: I was almost 5 the first time he quit drinking. My mother had threatened to leave him before, but this time she had packed our bags. There were four of us kids and another on the way. My mother would have had no choice but to go on welfare and somehow survive with us.

My father promised to stop drinking and see a psychologist. He even went to a couple of AA meetings and decided to stick with therapy. This worked for almost nine years. Things improved greatly financially. A couple of years later my mom and dad bought a piece of property and began to build their dream home.

About a year before we were able to move in, my dad started drinking again. He had become an everyday drinker. Instead of disappearing for a couple of weeks at a time, he now had the opportunity to drink all day. Any shouting that happened between him and my mother we kids chalked up to the added stress of building this huge house for us.

We moved in and a few months later I came home from school to find a realtor's lock on the house. When I asked my mother what was going on she said that they needed to show the house to figure out the value.

I had started drinking and taking drugs a few years before and was now beginning to get into trouble because of it. My brother, who is one year younger than me, started drinking. He and I got into all kinds of trouble over the next few years. Things were getting progressively worse, and I noticed that I never saw my dad anymore except at work.

My mom told me that my father was an alcoholic and that he was going to AA to try to stop drinking. My dad seemed like a good businessman, didn't get arrested and didn't beat my mom. In other words, he seemed normal. He was my first impression of an alcoholic.

My father knew that if he ever drank again he would lose everything. He jumped into AA with both feet. He was going to meetings, a lot of them, and things got better for him. My brother and I, on the other hand, couldn't stay out of trouble or the police station, and the two youngest boys were just trying to stay out of the way.

Just as I turned 18, I got into more trouble with my brother. Because I had no record, I got a fine. My brother was about to have to go to the training school (juvenile hall), but my dad got the judge to sentence him to AA instead. He started to go to meetings. After a couple of months, he told me he was going to give this sober thing a try. Who quits drinking when they're 17?

I took off to college for one semester, and when I came back my brother had turned into someone I barely recognized. He talked about being a good guy and wanting to get along with everyone.

What radical ideas were they filling his head with at those AA meetings? We had spent good quality partying time together. Now it seemed that AA was going to take him away from me. In his senior year he made the honor roll and he went off to college.

In the meantime my life was spinning quickly out of control. I ended up in a detox. It was not a pleasurable experience. They talked to me in great detail about my drinking, but I was convinced that my drinking was out of control because I was taking painkillers.

Still, when I left the detox I came to AA. A lot of people seemed to know my name and I began to understand what "saving a seat for me" meant. I stayed sober for three months and went out for a night. When I woke up in the morning I couldn't believe what had happened. I drank with little or no control. I had not done any drugs so that wasn't the problem. I was definitely an alcoholic. It was devastating.

I came to AA for the next six months but couldn't seem to stay sober for more than a couple of days. I never considered how hard that must have been for my dad and brother to watch until years later. I drank for the next three years with little or no thought to the consequences. I was going to die an alcoholic.

A lot of AAs tried to give me a message of hope, but I was lost. I did pay attention to a few people who talked to me about things they wanted to do in their life and then somehow did. I could argue about what people said but not about the way they lived. The difference between them and me was that they were sober. After three years I got into an accident and, to please my mother, I returned to AA. I knew I would end up drinking again. I was doomed.

I had several resentments against AA. In my mind, AA had turned my father into an old softy and my brother into a "tree hugger" who talked about walking the earth softly with God. What on earth happened to the hell-raiser I knew? But I couldn't deny that they were both much, much happier than when they were drinking.

What happened was that five older guys (my dad's friends) took me under their wing. None of them seemed impressed with what I had to say, and they were far less impressed with what I was thinking. They practiced ego deflation at depth on me. After six or seven months, a little bit of hope crept into my life. Maybe if I just continued to follow the suggestions that these guys were giving me, I could stay sober too.

Right after my first year I got a call from my youngest brother. He was away at college and found himself in some trouble. My other sober brother and I went to see him. His drinking was out of control and he wanted to stop. He was 18, and had watched what had happened to us and didn't want to go down that road. We took him to a meeting. When the semester was over and he returned home, we brought him around to the local meetings, where he began to get active. He talked about how hard it was to be honest when everyone knows your family and expects you to be as sober as they are.

A woman started coming to our group around the same time as my brother. She was a piece of work! She was in the middle of a messy divorce, worked as a waitress and bartender, and had attitude written all over her. I was sure that she was going to end up drinking and I wanted nothing to do with her. But after a year and a half we began to talk a little and found that we had much more in common than either of us thought. We began dating and eventually got married.

A few years after I'd come into the program, my sister began to let stories slip about how much her husband was drinking, and some problems that were beginning to pop up. His life had all the earmarks of an alcoholic life. Finally my sister had enough and asked him to leave. He decided to come to AA in the hopes of saving the marriage. Their relationship has gotten better. It still catches me off guard when we talk about how God works in our lives today. We never argue about the outcome of our surrender anymore.

A year after my father helped my brother-in-law into AA, my father got a call from my aunt: Would he be willing to talk with her new husband about his drinking? He didn't think going to AA was a bad thing. He just didn't see the point in it. Still, after talking with my father he began to attend a few meetings regularly. Shortly after that he stopped drinking. He continues to attend meetings and he no longer wants to drink. My sister-in-law also got sober over the next few years.

Then my daughter began to have troubles with alcohol. There were a few instances that worried me, but there is one I will always remember. I was at work on a Saturday when I got the call that she had been involved in a car accident and I needed to get to the trauma center as quickly as I could. My wife was just getting there as I arrived. We were told that the accident had happened late the night before and that my daughter was not waking up. Her head had struck a telephone pole; she had shattered her orbital bones and her face was swollen and cut all over.

We were scared beyond words and weren't prepared to handle any of this. When we went back to the waiting room to let the doctors work on her, we couldn't believe what was waiting for us. When my wife got the call, she had made two phone calls. One was to my office, and the other to a friend because she didn't think she could drive herself to the hospital.

In the waiting room were about 30 of our friends and family, ready to support us through this in any way they could. Two phone calls. Not a guy who was prone to tears at the time, I fell into their arms and let the tears come. I have never been more amazed at the power of the group than I was that morning. It also reminded me of the countless emergencies when my parents had to come see their son.

Our daughter healed in time, but her drinking continued to escalate. It was obvious to everyone that her drinking was out of control, but the last thing she wanted to do was go to AA. It broke my heart to know that the answer was so close to her.

I talked with my dad often about how much pain I must have put him through with my drinking. It seemed karma was working overtime in my life. We surrendered to the fact that we might have to watch her die.

At a July 4th picnic we got a call from her, asking for help. She came kicking and screaming into AA. It was so familiar to me that I couldn't breathe. I'd gotten sober by the skin of my teeth, and I had wanted it to be easier for my daughter. Again this brought me closer to my dad. All he told me was that I had to trust that AA and God could handle her.

Eventually, she asked one of our best friends to be her sponsor and started to work the Steps into her life. When she sits on our couch now it is to laugh. She has friends who are sober and she doesn't want to drink anymore. She still doesn't want to have to belong to AA, but recognizes the need for it. Recently she gave birth to our first grandchild. We could not be happier. This may be the first child born on either side of our family to sober parents. Our hope is that the legacy of alcoholism will stop here.

When I speak at meetings I usually wind it up by giving the legacy of sobriety that is my family. My father came to AA 31 years ago, heard a message of hope and recovery, and hasn't had to drink since. My brother came to AA when he was 17—27 years ago—and hasn't had to drink since. I am 23 years sober. My wife is 22 years sober. My other brother is 22 years sober. My brother-in-law is 18 years sober. My uncle is 17 years sober. My sister-in-law is 14 years sober. And my beautiful daughter is four years sober. That's 178 years around my dinner table.

Not all of my family has made it to our rooms. My aunt died from the devastation of her stomach and esophagus caused by her drinking. I buried my 42-year-old cousin on the night of my 17th anniversary.

His death was due to liver failure. Both had known of AA and had also watched what it could do for someone. It just wasn't enough for them to surrender.

I don't know what it is that has brought so many of my family to our Fellowship. I don't believe that God's grace extended to me and not to my cousin. I don't believe that all the people I have witnessed in AA who have died from this disease were any more or less capable of being honest with themselves. We are all broken. The key to accepting a spiritual way of life came from that brokenness in me. Without surrender I don't stand a chance.

I am always aware that people are watching to see if this AA thing really changes someone's life, or if we just white-knuckle it. I tell them that I grow more in love with my wife every day. We are beyond just being satisfied. I have keys to all my families' houses and we get together as often as we can. We are a loud bunch who love to sing and dance and laugh together. We never end a conversation without saying "I love you." We have more friends than we can readily spend time with.

I am living a life far beyond anything I ever dreamed possible.

Alan D.
Pascoag, Rhode Island

A Box of Pears
Grapevine Online Exclusive – September 2014

A few days ago, I was at a speaker meeting in which a woman named Lisa told her story. I didn't expect to hear anything more than I usually hear, which is always helpful in some small way. I didn't expect to be moved more so than I am usually moved. Lisa is half-Japanese. She grew up on Long Island. She is probably 20 years my senior. There's nothing terribly similar about our lives, and nothing stands out to me now as the reason I was drawn to her immediately, but I was. Something about her face was familiar, kind. She started to tell her story, and I was captivated. I could identify, of course, with a lot of her childhood angst and discomfort, but it was more than that.

Before I got sober, I could never really hear anyone. Now I could truly listen to other people. So, I listened to Lisa. She told how at 17 years old she gave up a child for adoption. She described the feelings she had after she gave birth and the child was taken from her. She said something like, "I felt that all the air had been taken out of me, away from me. I felt empty and alone. I was confused and afraid. I didn't know how to do anything, how to live."

I really heard her. I heard her, and I understood what she'd felt in those terrible moments. And I cried. I tried to dry my tears with one finger, instead smudging the mascara under my eyes. Lisa continued with her story.

I raised my hand to share. I don't share very often—not because I don't have joy to share or sadness for which I need support, but because I really do love to listen to my fellows. But this time, I felt a powerful need to share.

I told Lisa and the group that she had given me a great gift: the gift of sympathy. I told her that when I was an active alcoholic, I never felt sympathy. I never felt anything. Alcohol had numbed me for so many years. I didn't even understand what other people meant when they said they felt sympathy or empathy. I knew how to behave as if I felt those same things, but I didn't really feel them. I had, for various powerful reasons, kept feelings at a distance. I explained to Lisa, and to the group, that my biological mother, who had given me up for adoption at birth and whom I had never known, had tracked me down some years ago.

I had seven Bloody Marys before meeting her. She'd found me, and I was angry. She'd found me, and when we met, she asked me to forgive her, and I didn't say anything. I held on to my anger for a while, and then I let it fade into indifference. I let the relationship become one of occasional emails and the box of pears I sent her at Christmas.

Not once in the years since she found me—her name is Leslie—had I thought about what she had gone through when she gave me up. Not once did I try to put myself in her shoes. And then, I heard Lisa's story. I thanked her for that very precious gift, and I thanked the group and AA for giving me the ability to accept this gift. I cried. A lot. That evening, I wrote to my biological mother. I told her the whole story. I told her of my anger when she tracked me down, and I told her of my gratitude for AA and for Lisa. This is some of what I said to her in that letter:

"The truth? Being adopted has affected me in many ways, both good and bad. But I'm not writing to you about that today. I'm writing to you to say thank you for making the difficult choice to put me up for adoption. I am so grateful for the life I have had as a result. Until yesterday, I knew it had to have been difficult, but I never fully grasped the pain and fear you must have felt. So, there's this part of me now that wants to say, 'Let's really get to know each other.' There's this part of me that wants a hug from you so much, and to hug you right back. But there's this other part of me that is afraid. I am afraid. But I suppose I hope we can make some small steps forward. Maybe we can just start to email more often and maybe talk sometimes on the phone."

I would never have written that letter had I not learned about listening to other people and feeling sympathy for their circumstances.

Stephanie R.
Long Island, New York

My Father's AA
March 2005

F riends of my parents had a pool and they'd throw wild parties. My sisters, the other kids, and I would swim while the
parents drank. We knew they were all drunk when the singing started. My mother would get out her accordion and wake up my
father, who was usually passed out, and they would do their famous
duet of the Titanic song, a cheerful little ditty about disaster. "Husband and wives, little children lost their lives ..." with everyone joining in on the chorus of, "It was sad ..." The song kind of summed up
our family life. We were sinking fast.

When I was 12, I threw a little New Year's party up in my room
while my parents had a party in our basement. My buddies and I drank
vodka, scotch, and rum I'd smuggled up in baby jars. We were having
a great time until I decided I needed more. (The phenomenon of craving had set in, even then.) My father was actually relatively sober that
night and he knew instantly that I wasn't. He flew into a rage. "What
are our neighbors going to think when their kids come home from our
house drunk?" I wanted to tell him the neighbors knew all about us.
He was always coming home from work falling-down drunk and I'd
have to stop playing with my friends to help him inside.

My father felt that as long as he was making a good living, no one
could say anything about his drinking. But when I was 15, his company
gave him an ultimatum: Quit drinking or be fired. After a month in a
rehab he felt he knew all he needed to know and that he would quit
drinking on his own. He made it a couple of months. After the second
rehab, he got a sponsor and started going to meetings.

The palms of my father's hands used to turn red when he was tense
and they were red most of the time in those first months. Sundays were
particularly hard; he didn't know what to do with himself. Friends

of his from AA would drop by and that seemed to help. They were a strange bunch, often revealing degrading things about themselves and then laughing uproariously about them. And these people wouldn't disappear when there was trouble, like his old drinking pals did. Instead, they came by more often. Sometimes his sponsor and this old guy Walter (who everyone treated with reverence) would come for dinner on Sundays. Walter had been sober since 1942 and told good stories about the early days of AA. Then they'd all head off to the Sunday night meeting at the rehab and I'd head to my room to smoke dope.

For several years, I'd been smoking pot every day, using amphetamines to keep up with school work, and experimenting with LSD. However, it was nothing like my father's drinking. I wasn't trying to get stupefied. I was altering my consciousness. I practiced Transcendental Meditation and read books about Zen. I was on a quest for enlightenment.

The summer before college, I got a job at a nice restaurant where they taught me about fine wines. This was definitely different from my father's drinking: he was a shot-and-a-beer guy, I was a connoisseur. My first weekend at college, I introduced my new dormmates to sophisticated drinking—and promptly threw up all over the hall.

Adopting my father's former attitude, I thought that as long as I performed well in school, no one could hassle me about my drinking. My first semester I was an honor student and won a writing award. By junior year I was on academic probation. The blackouts got more frequent. But this was still not my father's drinking. I was studying writing, and drinking was a necessary part of the creative process. I drank what my favorite writers drank, but it didn't help me write like they wrote.

My father bought me a car so I could visit home on weekends. I racked up parking tickets and expected my father to pay them. The little things he went out of his way to do for me, I took for granted. Only occasionally would I stop and consider that he had completely changed his character. I remember being in his room one day and seeing the word "Communicate" posted on his mirror. My father? Wanting to communicate?

It started to become clear that I had a drinking problem. One Sunday morning, he got a call from the state police. My car was smashed up on the side of the highway. He ran downstairs to find me passed out in my bed with several cuts on my arms and head. Oh yeah, I'd hit a tree. I talked my way out of trouble with the police and minimized the whole thing. When he actually saw the wrecked car, it took his breath away. It was amazing that I had survived. I heard years later that he'd cried that night at the Sunday night meeting. By then I was already drunk again, and joking about it with my friends.

I told my parents not to come to my college graduation—I was too bohemian to bother with rituals like that. The truth was, I had several incompletes thanks to drinking. I moved in with my parents, telling myself that without the pressure of rent to pay, I could finish up my incompletes, graduate, and get on with my life. After a month I hadn't finished any papers, just lots of bottles. My father invited me to a restaurant for lunch and I steeled myself for the "get a job" speech. Instead, he told me his story. I remember that what sliced right through my denial was when he said that he hadn't gotten into trouble every time he drank, but every time he got into trouble, the bottle was behind it. He offered to send me to the same rehab he had gone to. I was too confused and beleaguered to say no. And I was curious. What if this was my problem? What if I wasn't an awful human being, just one who was sick with alcoholism?

Everyone at the rehab knew my father and was looking out for me. At the daily lectures, I learned about the disease concept, and in group I started to see how grandiose and self-centered I was. I went to the Sunday night meeting that my father had chaired off and on for years and when I moved back with my parents, my father and I went to meetings together. However, it was still "my father's AA," not mine, and I didn't try to make it mine by finding a sponsor or a home group where I fit in. Instead, I tried smoking pot, and days later I was drunk, too drunk to drive. I called home hoping to get my sister to come and pick me up. My father answered. I tried to disguise my voice, but it was clearly me, clearly drunk. He drove me home, not saying a word.

Several days before he'd written, "Meeting Makers Make It" on a chalk-board. I ripped it off the wall, then took a swing at him. Fortunately, I was so drunk that I was easily subdued.

I decided to move back to my college town and figure out this drinking thing on my own. My father knew it was a geographic, but he paid for my plane ticket and wished me luck. I had to get obliterated to stop the voice in my head that told me I had no business drinking. As bad as things got, I refused to go back to AA, but I did decide to try counseling. It was a study in half measures and it availed me nothing. I managed to put together three months of not drinking and told my father about it (leaving out the part about smoking pot every day). He sent me a three-month chip taped to the responsibility statement: "I am responsible. When anyone, anywhere reaches out, I want the hand of AA always to be there. And for that: I am responsible." His disclaimer: This isn't your father sending you this, it's a fellow AA member. Three months later, I got another chip.

Shortly after this, I learned that my father had liver cancer. I decided it was time to get my act together and forced myself to go to a meeting. Standing awkwardly by the coffee pot, I heard my name. I was sure it was someone from the rehab who'd been sober the last two years while I'd been getting wasted. It turned out to be my creative writing teacher from college. I was shocked to see him there. He wasn't at all surprised to see me. I would never have found the right sponsor, so the right sponsor found me. Here was a guy I couldn't snow with all my literary reasons for needing to drink. Here was a guy I knew was smarter than I, so when he said there was no mental defense against the first drink, I listened. He helped open my closed mind enough so I could at least try to pray.

That year, we all came home for the holidays. My mother sent us a photo beforehand so we wouldn't be shocked when we saw my father. His thick black hair was gone, his face had aged 20 years, and his arms and legs were like twigs. He and I went to meetings every day he felt up to it; we brought along a cushion so he'd feel more comfortable. It was a difficult Christmas. I still get choked up every year when I hear

Judy Garland sing those lyrics about being together, "if the fates allow."

A month later I came for another visit. While I'd only been clean for four months, it'd been a year since I'd had a drink. My sponsor told me that if my father wanted to celebrate, then I should do what made him happy. We went to his home group and he presented me with a one-year coin, the very one he'd gotten after his first year. He said it had a good track record.

On the drive home, he asked me to pull over. He opened the door and vomited. I figured he was still getting chemo, that sort of thing happens. Then I saw that he'd vomited blood. I was overwhelmed, but he kept a cool head and soon we were at the emergency room. It was very busy, and I couldn't get them to pay attention to us, but then he threw up more blood, and they quickly took him inside. I didn't know what to do or think so I just repeated the Serenity Prayer over and over. An hour later they told us that they didn't know why, but the bleeding had stopped, and we could come back and see him. He was propped up on a gurney, pale, but smoking a cigarette and smiling.

A day before I left, I asked if I could talk with him. I wasn't up to the Ninth Step yet, but I spoke to him about regretting the things I'd done that had hurt him. He told me not to worry about it—all was forgiven. I wanted to say more, but I got the feeling he couldn't handle any more emotion just then, any more sorrow or regret. Maybe we both could have had a good cry together. As it was, I did my crying staring out the window of the airplane, knowing I would never see him again.

At his memorial service, his AA friends were there, as they'd been for the last eight years. More than any other accomplishments in his life, his service to the Sunday night meeting and the hand he extended to the still-suffering alcoholic defined his life.

In the back of my mind I felt like I deserved to drink again. "Poor me, poor me, pour me a drink." If I'd talked about it to anyone, I might not have acted on it. But I kept quiet, went on a road trip with some work friends, drank again, and blacked out again. The next morning we passed within a mile of where he's buried. I thought to myself, The one thing he wanted for you was that you stay sober. Instead, you used your feelings about him to justify drinking, and within 24 hours you were as bad as ever. What is that if not powerless? After one more "convincer" I finally became willing to do whatever it took. I actually did some of the things my sponsor suggested, and started telling him when something was bothering me instead of storing it away for the next time I needed an excuse to drink. I began doing service and worked the Steps.

On my first real anniversary, I dug out the coin he'd given me and said a prayer of thanks. For my next eight anniversaries, my mother would send me another one of his coins, and I'd feel a deep sense of connection with him. I went to the AA Archives in New York and looked at a photo from the 1980 International Convention in New Orleans. He was there, somewhere in the crowd. I've been to the last few and I feel like he's there with me.

Last year, I was helping my mother go through some old boxes and I ran across a cassette tape that said, "Walter's Talk." A chance to hear more of Walter's stories about the early days. I decided to play it on my upcoming anniversary. That night, after a joyous celebration at my home group, I put the tape into a player, relaxed into my favorite chair, and prepared to hear Walter. But the first voice on the tape wasn't Walter's, it was my father's. He was chairing the meeting. As I listened to him recite the Preamble, tears welled up in my eyes. My 12-year-old came in. "Is that ... your father?" I nodded and he sat down next to me. We listened as my dad told the crowd at the Sunday night meeting they were in for a treat. I felt the hand of AA and the hand of my father reach across the years. It was there for me, just the way he always wanted it to be.

J. W.

Maplewood, New Jersey

I Stole the Wallet

August 2010

When I grew up I had a favorite uncle whom I've come to believe was an alcoholic, just like me. I was always excited to be around this uncle. He drank and seemed to have a lot of fun. At one time, he was a deputy sheriff, and so he knew everyone from one end of the county to the other. The first time I drank was with him, and the first time I got really drunk was with him—at the ripe old age of 11.

I was 18 years old when I was drunk one Sunday night and broke, so I drove up to his place to see if I could borrow some money. I found both him and a man who was living with him passed out. I stole the wallet of the man living with him and left the house unnoticed.

This man blamed my uncle for stealing his money. The sheriff was called in. My uncle had worked for him and had drunk himself out of that job. It was very embarrassing and shameful for my uncle to go through that. Eventually, it blew over.

I left for the Marine Corps and tried to forget about the incident, but every now and then when I was back home I would think about it when I ran into my uncle. I felt a lot of guilt and shame when it came up in my thoughts, and I drank to make it go away. It was like a monkey on my back.

When I sobered up and was in treatment, this came up in my Fourth and Fifth Steps, so obviously it was on my Eighth Step list. It was meant to clear up the wreckage of my past so I didn't have to have it haunt me for the rest of my life.

My uncle, although a fun-loving man, had a very volatile temper. I was scared, to say the least, but I knew I had to make that amends. I met with him on a Saturday morning in his garage and brought up the incident. He remembered it as though it were yesterday. I told him that I was the one who stole the money. Believe me, I was extremely uncomfortable. It was very awkward for both of us. I was, you could say, the apple of his eye and we had done many things together, so it really threw him for a loop. I asked my uncle for forgiveness and told him I was very sorry for the misery I had caused him.

He looked me right in the eye and said, "Lee, what's between us is between us, and that's the end of it." When I walked out of that garage I was a free man, released of the bondage of self. This gave me faith that I was on the right path and that this AA business worked.

Years later this same uncle was in an assisted care home. He needed help with his affairs but was strongly rejecting help, even from a very close brother, another uncle of mine. This other uncle asked me to help him. I met with my first uncle and told him we loved him and wanted to help him, but we needed his help to go through a power of attorney hearing. With much skepticism on the part of a court administrator and others, the next day we had the proceeding. I prayed for the strength to go through with this and was prepared for the worst, but everything went without a hitch and people walked out of the room shaking their heads. I put my arms around my uncle and just cried. I know that when I made that amends to him years before he knew I wouldn't lie to him and he trusted me to do the right thing. Six months later he passed away and my other uncle was able to handle the estate without any glitches. There's only one way this would have happened and that is with God's help and guidance.

Lee C. J.

Fargo, North Dakota

Cartoons and Bourbon
March 2014

My dad brought me home from the hospital on Sept. 19, 1960. I was five days old. On the way, he had to stop at an old hotel bar. If you were from "The Bottoms," outside of Pittsburgh, you knew of this place. It was an old saloon, now long torn down. I remember Dad telling me that he facetiously baptized me by dabbing his thumb into a shot glass of bourbon. He made the sign of the cross as I whined, then stuck that thumb in my mouth.

As I got older, I would go with my dad whenever he went to that old hotel. He'd drink double shots of bourbon, and I would sit and watch the cartoons. Often he would leave a little bit in the shot glass for me. They would play that Stealers Wheel song "Stuck in the Middle with You." I remember it because the guy was singing about being scared of falling off his chair and wondering how he'll get down the stairs … "clowns to the left of me, jokers to the right." Drunk on bourbon, I'd stagger back to my little table to watch more cartoons.

By the time I was 5, I was drinking every Saturday. In fact I got so good (as if getting good at drinking is an accomplishment) that my dad would make bets with men at the bar about how much I could drink. He'd make money that way. If I lost the bet, sometimes he'd leave me at the bar and the waitress would take me home, and he'd come pick me up in the morning at her house. Dad was an angry and violent drunk and would often go home and beat up my mom or my brother.

He always used the rent money for booze, but my mom suffered from cerebral palsy so she couldn't stand up to him. So many times he would wake us at 2:00 in the morning and say, "The moving truck is here." I guess going to 14 schools in five years is a telling sign that the moving truck was around a lot. Finally my mom got up the nerve to leave him. She got bus tickets for herself and the six children and we moved to the west coast.

As a teenager I moved back to the east coast for a bit to live with my dad to go to high school. He hadn't changed much. He and I lived above a bar and then over an adult bookstore.

After many years of drinking, in March of 1992 I finally made it to AA—thanks to the guidance, love and direction of some members of my family. The following November, my grandparents were having their 50th wedding anniversary. Not yet being of sound mind, I decided it would be a great idea to test my sobriety and drive back home to Pennsylvania to see them. Maybe part of me wanted to see my dad too. I hadn't seen him in years.

The anniversary party was awesome. The next day I called my cousin and told him I wanted to go see my dad. We went to my aunt's house, and she told me where I could find him. He lived in an old building, and as my cousin and I walked up the stairs, my cousin asked, "What are you going to do—hit him?" I just looked back and shrugged and said, "I don't know." We got to his apartment and I knocked on the door.

My dad opened the door. He looked right at me and said, "Can I help you?" I was so mad that he didn't recognize me that I wanted to hit him. After a couple of minutes he looked at me again and said, "Gene!" Then I said, "Yeah, dad, it's me." He hugged me for what seemed like an eternity and invited us into his apartment. I was overwhelmed by what I saw.

There were clean dishes. The heat was on. The electricity was on. The windows were clean. The pictures were neat and organized. My Navy picture was on his mantle. I had never sent it to him; my mom must have sent it. We sat down on his couch. As we talked, I saw a sparkle in his eye that I hadn't seen in forever. I just blurted out, "So Dad ... how long you been sober?"

He smiled. "I just celebrated seven months," he said. "Why do you ask?" He then reached out his hand toward my face. I didn't flinch as I had done in the past. My face was all wet. As he wiped away the tears he asked, "What's wrong?"

Here was this man who never cared or showed any affection to me reaching out tenderly with affection and compassion. I told him I too was celebrating six months of sobriety, and we talked at length about what AA had given us both so far and the lengths we would go to keep it.

Just then there was a knock on the door. I got up and answered it. It was my aunt. She joined us and said she wanted me to see for myself how much my dad had changed. Before I left I told him that he had a couple of grandsons who would love to know they have a grandpa. He assured me he would call me and we could arrange something.

I was so excited to drive home and share the news with my family. I told them everything. A few days later I went to class, and it was also my day to volunteer at the VA hospital. While I was working, I got a call telling me that my dad had died from cirrhosis. I cried for almost an hour. Then I remembered something my dad had said to me only a few days before: "You know son, only when I was able to let go was I ever able to get a grip."

We can't change the things that happen in our sobriety any more than we can change the things that happen when we drink. We just stay close to AA and the program so we don't go out there and drink.

Anonymous

Letting Go in Florida
March 2014

Desperation drove me into the rooms of AA on July 10, 1983. It was not my first attempt. I had gotten three months together, moved to Florida, and once again became the important, self-sufficient person I always thought I was. After a year of more drinking, I got fired from my job and was about to become homeless. The desperate can be sweetly willing. So when I finally made it into the rooms, I had no doubts this time. I got old-fashioned, no-nonsense AA, and a lot of love from the old-timers. But this story is not all about me.

I had four grown children at the time, all of them out there in party-land, Florida. They had followed me after my move. I did know enough not to enable them, but I also was so self-centered that, of course, it was still all about me. So I let them each stay with me for three months, until they found a job and an apartment. I'm blessed because I never lost my relationships with my kids. I didn't start alcoholic drinking until I was in my 30s, so thankfully we had developed a foundation with each other.

Thankfully, I heard my sponsor when she told me my children had their own disease, and that I was powerless over it. She instructed me to just keep doing what I was doing for my own sobriety—and to be an example. I used to drink with them, but by this time they were doing their own thing. I did coerce them into coming to my AA meeting each year when I picked up my anniversary medallion. They would sit there wondering which ones were alcoholics and which ones were there to support someone. But that was OK. They saw things and heard things.

My party-girl daughter (just like her mother) decided she'd make more money waitressing at a bar than in her office job. My oldest son was in the Army in Germany, and my youngest son didn't present many problems. But my youngest daughter was out there somewhere; every now and then she would come and stay over for the night. I knew that my oldest daughter was getting more and more into the 24-hour Florida nightlife. She was losing her car and doing some of the things that alcoholics do. So I prayed and prayed and prayed for her.

No, there was no miracle. But one night when I was four years sober, I got a phone call from her at 11 P.M. She said, "Mom, I think I have a problem with drinking." So I asked her to come over. When she got home, my 26-year-old daughter sat on my lap and cried. We hugged each other until she stopped crying. The next morning I took her to a meeting, introduced her to another woman and left.

I had been around long enough to know that I had to let her go. I knew I had to do it for the sake of my own sobriety and sanity, but mostly for hers. Boy, did I stick with my sponsor. My daughter went out briefly for some more experimenting; today she's 26 years sober.

My Army son had now moved to New York with his family. I found out about his alcoholic drinking when his wife left him and took the kids back to Germany. By now we were all down in Florida, so he followed us. In one conversation, after he mentioned how things had gone the night before and that the "bottle clubs" were going to get him, I said, "You might want to be careful before the bottle gets you." Like a good alcoholic, he said, "I know, I know, mom."

About six months later he was sitting in front of me, hungover and jobless, and I simply said, "Maybe you should take a look at your drinking." This time, in a different tone he said, "Mom, I've been wanting to talk to you about that." I took him to a meeting that night, pointed to a chair, and said, "That chair's yours; you've earned it." Then I introduced him to some guys and left. That was in 1988. When he was seven years sober he remarried and moved to Pennsylvania where his wife was from. Strangely enough, he didn't like the meetings, people weren't as friendly, etc., etc. So he went out for a couple of years. A DUI brought him back in. Today he has 17 years sober and he's a good husband and father. Thank you, God.

My youngest daughter has been around the program since about 1988. She stayed around for 15 years and had a daughter. Most of the time she didn't have a sponsor or a home group. Then she went out for several years. All I could do was pray. A year ago she got a DUI. But her denial was at its peak. This past Christmas she got another one and spent almost a month in jail. I believe that was God doing for her what she could not do for herself. She's now seven months sober and swears she's thrown in the towel. I love seeing her smile today. She's living with her sober older sister, who also has gone to some Al-Anon meetings. A day at a time they're mending their relationship, which was pretty damaged.

I have another wonderful son who happens not to be an alcoholic. He too drank and partied with the rest of us. But he stopped, turned to faith and walks the walk. Today he's a wonderful husband and father, and an elder in his church.

The time came for me to leave Florida. I moved to Pennsylvania five years ago. God was there before I arrived: he had gotten everything ready for me—my home, my sponsor, my home group and even a part-time job four blocks from where I live. How good is he?

My oldest daughter, who is 26 years sober and has been divorced since 1989, has had a few relationships that were all learning experiences. She kept on keeping on, and a couple of years ago she met Mr. Right, who has 27 years sober. This August when I went to Florida, they got married. She asked her 17-year sober brother to give her away and her seven-month sober sister to be her maid of honor. What a joy.

Three of my children and their families are still in Florida, so every summer we have a family reunion down there for a couple of weeks. I also meet with my old friends and sponsor, and pack my heart full of wonderful memories and gratitude.

So here we are. My children and I today total 73 years of sobriety—and now with my new son-in-law, the total is 100 years! Is that a fairytale or what? It's been hard work practicing letting go, and each giving away what we've so generously been given. We stay out of each others' programs and "live and let live." Each one of us has learned to live life on life's terms without picking up a drink or a drug.

We love our lives and our time together. I have 10 grandchildren, most of whom have never seen their parents drunk—and certainly can't imagine their grandmother drunk! What a blessing. I have sponsees here in Pennsylvania, I make plenty of meetings and I love fellowshipping with the ladies. It gets better and better. And when you think it can't get any better, it gets better.

Jeanne R.
Monaca, Pennsylvania

Struck Sober
August 2010

was struck sober 25 years ago in my oldest brother's attic, at 6:07 A.M., the moment of sunrise. I know the time and place because it was the single most important moment of my life, and the beginning of the road to recovery. God said to me, "Everything is going to be all right. The only thing you have to do is never take another drink or drug again." The light slowly faded and 15 years of physical compulsion and mental obsession with inebriation was lifted.

My brother had bailed me out of jail the night before. I'd been arrested one mile from town, after a 1,000-mile journey, for my fifth DUI. "I only had two beers!" I'd protested. I wanted to be dropped off at home to blow my head off with my deer rifle (which my brother didn't know, but may have suspected). Instead, he took me to his home, where the family had a meeting about my grave situation and my need to go into a treatment center. I attended my first AA meeting the next day, where I heard my story, met my sponsor and began my journey to freedom. A strange man came up to me, told me I stank, and said I needed to get into the nearby river and wash myself—which, amazingly, I did. He later became my sponsor.

My story is one of family disease—and family recovery. I am the youngest of four brothers; two who'd been sober nearly two years when I hit bottom, and another who got sober a year after me. We covered the gamut: country-club highroller, successful businessman, genius artist and juvenile delinquent. We subjected our parents to two decades of insane alcoholic behavior in the fishbowl of small-town America. We were well-educated, successful and admired on one hand; despised, loathed and pitied on the other. The embarrassment we caused ourselves in the community and the insanity we endured at family functions, with four raging alcoholic brothers, was tragic.

One by one, we crashed into the rooms of Alcoholics Anonymous and we recovered by practicing the principles of the program. We got sponsors, worked the Steps, did service work and had spiritual awakenings that removed the obsession to drink. My mother and little sister found peace and recovery in Al-Anon. Today, I honor my best friends— my three brothers—for trudging this road of happy destiny with me. I also have a nephew in recovery, which proves that the disease lives on even as we tried to break the chain in our generation.

Our sobriety proves that AA works. God willing, this year my three brothers and I will celebrate 100 years of collective continuous sobriety.

Kirk K.

Al Ain, United Arab Emirates

Game Changer

December 2010

My father was my hero. Actually, he still is, even though he passed away in November of 2005. He was a man of great character and integrity and had an incredible sense of humor, which he maintained right up to the very end of his life. Shortly before he died, when he was in the final stages of emphysema and struggling to breathe, my mother tried to comfort him. "Joe, we are so lucky," she whispered (speaking of the 43 years of marriage they had shared). He just looked up and without missing a beat remarked, "Yeah, if I could breathe, I'd be whistling."

That was my father, quick-witted and always with a smile on his face. He could make me laugh at the drop of a hat, and our daily phone calls always consisted of lots of funny stories and lots of love.

It wasn't always that way. Growing up as the only girl with three younger brothers, I found plenty to complain about. Our family life revolved around sports, particularly hockey and baseball. My father would make sure he made every Little League game and hockey practice for each of "the boys" and it seemed like our lives revolved around tryouts, practices and games. The missed dinners, the countless weekend afternoons spent on baseball fields and hockey rinks made me very resentful and jealous. I felt like the odd girl out. As a rebellious teenager who knew it all, I staged my own personal baseball strike. I stopped going to the games and avoided family dinner time altogether.

Eventually, somewhere along the line, things between me and my dad improved. We began to get closer and even began talking, I mean really talking with each other. Growing up and maturing has a way of doing that. Or maybe it was when he stopped drinking—or when I did. I sort of think it was a combination of it all. One thing is for sure, the end of "our" drinking definitely played a huge role in this transformation.

As a young girl, my father's drinking had an enormous affect on me. I hated Friday nights because he would head straight to the bar with his friends and not come home until 3 or 4 in the morning. All through the night, I would keep peeking out my bedroom window, to see if his car was in the driveway yet. The vision of the empty driveway still fills my heart with pain. Eventually, he would make his way home and I would then wake up to the sounds of him and my mother yelling at each other in the kitchen. Even though I would cover my head with my pillow to block out the tearful pleas of my mother, these arguments penetrated my soul.

I know it sounds terrible, but I was ashamed of my father's drunken behavior. I grew up watching "The Brady Bunch," and Mike Brady certainly never behaved this way. I was so embarrassed by this and could not share it with anyone, not even my best friend. She came from the perfect family. Her father was a lawyer and they lived on the nice side of town (actually, her father ended up representing my father on several of his DUIs—so I guess the secret was out anyway).

I did not like the person my dad became when he drank. He wasn't violent or abusive, but he just wasn't himself. I would cringe at family gatherings when he picked up that first drink. I knew that one always led to another, and another, and another. He was funny and entertaining for a short time, but then always became sloppy and I would get annoyed. Although I loved my father deeply, I didn't like to be around him when he drank.

And then he stopped drinking. To be honest, I do not remember the exact date when my father decided to stop or what events led to it. What I do remember is that all of sudden he was not drinking anymore. There were no proclamations, no intervention, no rehab—he just stopped. I guess enough had become enough. Although his decision was evidently a private one, it had a tremendous impact on my entire family. The embarrassment and shame was replaced with deep love, respect and affection. As a sober man, he was all that I could ever hope a father would be (and put Mike Brady to shame!).

Unfortunately, things had not gotten completely better, because I had started drinking. At first, it was just because all my friends were doing it, but pretty quickly it became apparent that I drank differently from my friends. I now know that I was born with this genetic predisposition to alcoholism, but for years I believed that I was just a girl who liked to party hard. And, boy, did I ever. Over the next 20-something years, my drinking went from something I did socially, to loosen up and enjoy myself, to something I needed to do every night just to calm my nerves. It was no longer an option, it was a necessity.

In June of 2001 my father had a talk with me. He told me how concerned he was about my drinking and that I needed to stop. I felt numb. I couldn't believe he had just addressed the elephant in the room. I thought I had hidden it so well from my family; obviously I hadn't. And one of the most powerful moments during that conversation was the realization that here I was—the one who was so ashamed of him when he was a dopey drunk—having to face the reality that I was now the one filling that role. I was filled with shame and remorse.

About a month later I went to my first AA meeting. That date—July 15, 2001—has become one of the most important dates in my life. Immediately after that first meeting I called my father. I was crying, but I also felt like a huge weight was off my shoulders. His birthday had been the day before, and when I told him where I had just been he said, "You don't have to give me another birthday present for the rest of my life."

Sobriety brought us even closer. We talked almost every day and he was my biggest supporter in this new life. During my first 90 days he counted every day with me. He would constantly tell me how proud he was of me (something I never remember from my childhood) and I can't even count the number of times he said, "You've come a long way, baby!" We were no longer hiding behind the alcohol; we were experiencing love, pure and simple—and it was because we were both sober.

Sobriety taught me many things. First and foremost, I learned that alcoholism was indeed a disease, not a moral weakness. I also learned about compassion, that you could "love the person and not the disease." I eventually realized that all those times I was embarrassed by my father's drinking and behavior (and my own, for that matter), it was actually the effects of the alcohol that I couldn't stand. I had always loved the person underneath.

In the fall of 2005, while I was visiting my parents, my father told me that he'd had a dream about his funeral, and that he had written the eulogy. When I asked him for details, he didn't want to talk about it (we were still dancing around the whole death conversation). A few minutes later he said, "OK, I'll tell you part of it. My life has been like a baseball game—I had good innings, and bad innings, and I found God in the bottom of the ninth."

I was floored by this spiritual revelation from a man who did not attend church and never really talked about God. It became apparent that as he moved closer to his own death, he had finally reached out and found what he needed to process this whole experience. Of course, what didn't surprise me was the sports analogy—that was classic "Joe."

My father passed away a few weeks later. Losing my hero was devastating, but I found great comfort and solace in the fact that he had made a spiritual connection prior to his death. This helped immensely during the days and weeks that followed. Knowing that he had come to terms with his own mortality helped me accept it as well. It also helped me stay sober. I had always thought that when my father died, I would have to get drunk. When that day did come I didn't have the slightest desire to pick up a drink, which in itself was miraculous. I also knew that there wasn't enough wine in California to take away the pain, and that drinking would just make it all worse.

It is coming up on three-and-a-half years since his death, and not a day goes by that I don't think about my father. Often I find it hard to believe that he has been gone this long, but I have so many wonderful memories of him, and they always bring a smile to my face. I guess I have come to terms with his death, but I still miss him terribly. And while I know it sounds funny coming from a girl who grew up hating sports, what I wouldn't give for extra innings with him.

Susan B.

Alexandria, Virginia

How My Child Came to Believe

August 1962

One of the most poignant and least communicated experiences of the alcoholic's life is the loss of children due to a marriage breakdown caused by alcoholism. I am a mother who lost my son during the final months of my drinking and I am a mother who has regained not only the physical custody of my child but the respect and affection of his father. Of all the blessings AA has bestowed this is surely the most deeply felt and the greatest daily reminder of the gratitude I owe to this Fellowship.

My experience is far from unique and not all of these tragic separations have such a happy ending. But after many discussions with both AA mothers and fathers I have come to know that there need never be a permanent separation from any child no matter how alienated the parents may be. Few parents, regardless of how bitter their personal relations may be, wish to be responsible for the unhappy results of separating a son or daughter from a father or mother who has returned to the human community through the healing influence of the AA life.

The most difficult attribute to acquire in this most painful situation is patience. When I first came into AA I was told by my non-AA attorney and by many newer AA friends that the courts were knowledgeable and lenient with parents who could prove their "fitness" through AA rehabilitation. I would have little or no legal trouble re-establishing my "rights," they assured me. I thank God every day of my life that I took the much harder course advocated by an AA attorney friend with some good long years of AA wisdom behind him.

I'll never forget what he said: "Rights? Oh sure, you have a legal right, but what is your spiritual right just now? If you insist on one before you understand the other you might well cause even deeper damage to your son and to yourself. If you wait until AA has had a chance, until you are aware of your total commitment to and responsibility for your sobriety, you may never have to go to court. You may also gain more, far more, than you ever had before."

I waited—two long and pretty appalling years, seeing my young son only under the watchful and hostile surveillance of his stepmother. I had to watch his confusion and unhappiness and his questions had to be answered, "Why can't I be with you?"; "Why were you away so long?"; "Why do I have to be with Daddy?"

I had to answer and I had to say, "I do not know how long it will be until your Daddy is able to share you. We will both have to wait and know that this is necessary now. You are not *away* from me really."

Finally the day did come when his father came to believe, through what he had learned of AA and what he had seen in me, that I was the one with the greater "fitness." Our son could now grow far stronger under the influence of what this program could bring to his life than through the climate in which his father operated. My son is nearly ready for college now, and he is indeed AA oriented, which means he is healthy in mind and spirit and strong in a conviction of God.

I know it does not always work this way—but children grow up. Any sober contact, no matter how brief and unsatisfactory, is better than association with the sickness of the actively drinking parent. In time the child will come to know the truth no matter how distortedly it has been presented to him or her. I believe deeply that the alcoholic parent is wrong even when right, until AA time has cast its sobering and healing spell. I also believe that the power of the love that AA can unfold for us is stronger and wiser than any court edict. Time, if we but give it, will in the end not only restore but sanctify.

I have since discussed this matter with my son's father. He said, "You wrote to me that you would never go to court to do battle for our son, even though you might lose him. When you said you'd wait until he was old enough to understand, I knew I could trust you." Great indeed are the rewards of AA's gifts of love and patience and willingness to let God's time, not ours, determine the way to actions of balanced sanity.

H. W.
New York, New York

Oil and Water
April 2007

Resentment truly is the "number-one offender." I was enlightened to this fact only one month ago. I had a resentment of 24 years concerning my sister-in-law that, in my 13 years of sobriety, I thought I'd "dealt" with.

I can laugh at myself now, and wonder, How could I think that I was OK with an individual and yet feel a stab of annoyance or anger at the mention of their name? How could I think everything was all right? I also found it strange that most of the resentments that festered have concerned people I care about and love.

The resentment with my sister-in-law was a "sticking point" in my growth, even though I denied it. Most of it stemmed from her relationship with my mother and my youngest sister—stormy, hurtful relationships within our family dynamics easily brought out the negative aspects of my personality. My husband remarked that my resentment was actually with myself, for I had done nothing to try to bring peace between my warring family members. He told me that there was nothing I could do to change what they said and did, that I could only change myself. His words opened up something in my heart.

Ten months ago, my mother's death triggered something in me. Before she died, she forgave her daughter-in-law. I was happy for the two of them, and in the weeks following her death, I came across some of her writing. God sent me a message on that day, written in my mother's shaky script. I cried when I read it. She wrote, "Forgiveness is a decision—forgive with your heart, not just with words." I realized how empty my amends to my sister-in-law had been. I never forgave her with my heart, only with empty words.

One day, my resentment reached its boiling point. A confrontation between us occurred. Although I kept my tongue civil and, according to my husband, behaved admirably well, my sister-in-law said and did some hurtful things to my younger sister and me. I stewed and brewed and a major rift began to form in our family. Someone had to take the first step and stop it.

For 13 days, I anguished and struggled. I prayed. I lost 10 pounds and lots of sleep. On the evening of the 13th day of the "cold war," as I was preparing supper, my mind once again strayed to thoughts of my sister-in-law. In my mind, I composed a mental list consisting of two columns. One column listed all the nice things she had done for me over the years; the second column was the list of nice things I had done for her. Surprise! Column one was much longer than column two. I felt suddenly very ashamed. I began thinking about all the qualities in her that I admired—there were many. Another realization dawned on me: I was envious of those qualities. I felt extremely foolish. I thought very hard about how I would feel if I were in her shoes and had to deal with me all these years. I felt the pain she must have felt.

Mentally, I began composing a letter to her. I covered all the good things she had put in my life, and, within an instant of starting it, the resentment vanished. I felt it leave me. I was so grateful; I cried and thanked God.

That night, I pondered the best way to make amends. I needn't have bothered, because God planned it for me. The very next day, she was put in my path. My husband and I were at my mom's house taking some of our things from the garage, when my sister-in-law showed up with her father. Coincidence? I don't believe that at all. She walked to our truck and handed a box of old family photographs to my husband. She looked older and more tired since I'd last seen her. As she turned to walk away, I called her by name and said, "I'm so sorry I hurt you." I'll never forget what ensued. Her face crumpled like a dried leaf and she turned away in tears. I jumped out of the truck and hugged her and told her that I loved her, that she was a good person, and mostly that I was sorry I was such a terrible sister-in-law. What a sight for the neighbors—two menopausal women standing in the falling snow, hugging and crying, then laughing and talking.

Now, when I think of my sister-in-law or hear her name mentioned, I get a good feeling—love instead of anger or jealousy. Our personalities may be like oil and water; they do not mix well. But now I see the symbiotic relationship of the oil and the water. The oil needs the water to support it, just as the water needs the oil to demonstrate its ability to hold something on its surface.

So, while resentment is the number-one offender, it has also been my best teacher. I have learned painfully (the way I always seem to learn) that forgiving with words is not enough for my peace of mind. I must forgive entirely, with my heart and with my soul, not just with my mind.

The 13th year of my sobriety was the most emotionally wrenching year of my recovery. During this year, I watched my mother die and now I'm watching a dear friend die of the same disease. In addition, my uncle had a paralyzing stroke, and I went blind in my left eye.

I asked God, "Why is all this awful stuff happening?" In the ensuing silence, the realization came to me: Only now, at this point in my life, can I accept it all and learn. A year ago, perhaps, I wouldn't have made it through. I realized how much good there is in people, including myself.

My love and gratitude runs too deep to be expressed in words. So, I will end with one of my favorite quotes from one of my meditation books. Most apropos, the author is Anonymous: "I came into AA to save my ass and found that it was attached to my soul."

Lorraine P.
Schreiber, Ontario

A Letter Every Week

December 2014

My dad and I have always had a fairly emotionless relationship. Before I got sober, I couldn't really express anything other than silent anger toward him for not being the dad that I wanted him to be. In return, he was void of emotion because of his own relationship with alcohol. When I got sober, he of course wound up on my Eighth Step list, but it wasn't until I was nearly six years sober that I actually did something about the amends.

When my sponsor, Kathy, and I were going through my list, we came to my dad. I can count on one hand the number of times that my father has picked up the phone and called me during my nearly 30 years of existence—and that's only part of what makes me mad. So she gave me this instruction: "I want you to write your dad a letter every week and let him know how you're doing." I immediately thought that was the dumbest thing I'd ever heard, but I didn't tell her that. "Does it have to be long?" I asked. "No," she said. "Just write to him about what's going on in your life."

It sounded doable, and so my amends began. Every week, I wrote a little something about what was going on at work, what my plans were for the weekend, or a good movie I had seen. It didn't take much time, and I had his address at the assisted living home memorized. When I talked to him on the phone, he never mentioned the letters; nor did I. My self-centeredness half expected a letter back from him in the mail, thanking me for taking the time to write him every week, but nothing of the sort ever happened.

About a year or so went by, and I got a package in the mail that had his aggressive handwriting on the front, even though it looked a little older and a bit shakier than I remembered. I opened it up to find stationary. Nothing else ... just a couple of packages of note cards and envelopes. No handwritten note from him saying, "Hey, Robyn. Thanks for all the notes you've written me. Keep them coming. Love, Dad." Nope. And I realized that I was totally OK with that. I loved it. Over the next couple of years, I got a few more packages of stationary, all of them just like the first one. Full of hope, I felt the anger toward my dad melting. The spiritual life is not a theory. We have to live it, right?

In October 2010, I got a call that my dad had passed away suddenly from a stroke in the middle of the night. Over the course of the next few days, my siblings and I cleaned out his apartment, and I was given the duty of cleaning off his desk. As I went through his mounds of receipts and papers, I kept coming across the letters I had written him. "Can't wait to see you next week at our wedding!" one said. "School is almost out—it's been a long year," said another. One of the more recent ones read, "Tomorrow is my first prenatal appointment!!"

With tears of sadness, I kept cleaning up. And then I came across several packages of stationary lying there on his desk, waiting to be packaged up and sent to me. My heart welled up and a huge smile spread across my face. I realized right then that, despite our inability to communicate our love face-to-face or over the phone, our relationship began healing from the moment that Kathy gave me direction over three years ago. Thirty years of damage from drinking was slowly repaired by following a very simple task from my sponsor.

And as if to remind me of where to direct my gratitude, there buried under a bunch of papers was his copy of *Alcoholics Anonymous*. I tucked my notes inside it. It now sits on my bookshelf, reminding me of the power of the Ninth Step of our simple, but never boring, program of recovery.

Robyn W.
Cincinnati, Ohio

CHAPTER TWO

Marriage and Divorce

We don't have to drink over love, or the loss of it

ove, honor and betray: Alcohol takes the same toll on a marriage as it does on a person. In the story "Are AA Marriages Different?" K.N. writes that "emotionally and spiritually, we do have an edge." Though the cap may still be left off the toothpaste and the hamper may be missed by a mile, relationship challenges are shared with sponsors, taken to meetings or aired soberly with each other. "We call on AA and our Higher Power," she writes, "and to date they have not failed us."

In Donna M's "A Love Story," an unborn baby is a casualty of the little-known effects of alcohol on pregnancy. In "Marriage—Drunk and Sober," scholars Jan and Fran P. drank till they passed out on their wedding night, kept it up, and never knew each other sober. Their brainy, accomplished married life got smaller and smaller until the miracle of sobriety offered them decades of simple happiness.

The stories in this chapter offer a dramatic picture of married life before and after alcohol made it a threesome. In the story "Marriage," by J.L., a sponsor's advice saves that union, but only after a painful, instructive separation. What happens if you marry a drunk and then fall in love with his sober version? asks J.D.G. in "Love Story." The Steps work, Robert M. learns in "Finding Love Again on AA Campus," to prevent us from falling in love with our old fantasies, habits, and self-sabotage, making grownup marriages possible.

Are AA Marriages Different?

January 1983

We got sober in AA, met in AA, and married in AA—second time for each of us. How different is an AA marriage?

Well—not to take my husband's inventory—he leaves the cap off the toothpaste, throws clothing on top of the hamper and not in it, and is often glued to the TV set watching sports. It's not physically different, is it?

Emotionally and spiritually, though, I think we do have an edge. When we get angry with each other, we can share it with a sponsor or attend a meeting. We always feel better afterward, and the disagreement usually fades away. Because of AA, we can also share our feelings with each other—whether happiness, sadness, anger, or love—without guilt.

We enjoy attending meetings, together as well as separately. We each have our own program, working it our own way. We do not always agree on certain things in the program, but we listen to each other's views.

At times, we have family problems, since his boys and mine all live in our home. I hear the "ideal" second marriage should be a *blending* of families; ours is sometimes more like La Machine. That is when we call on AA and our Higher Power, and to date they have not failed us.

K. N.
Newtown Square, Pennsylvania

Marriage—Drunk and Sober

February 2003

L ooking back, it's obvious that alcohol was always central in our relationship. We met, drinking, in college, and got engaged and married, drinking. Our wedding night, we drank until we passed out, and hungover, we left on our honeymoon, driving to a new life in California, each holding a can of cold beer between our legs.

Graduate school was a perfect setting for us. We soon had a group of friends who saw the world as we did and drank as we did. The next four years were filled with parties and a sense of our intellectual superiority. We didn't have much money, but there was always money to drink, partly because we established credit at a grocery store that sold beer and wine.

After completing the course work for the Ph.D. in English, my husband, Fran, was offered a teaching position at the University of Arizona. Life in the desert seemed made for the kind of drinking we now were doing. The weather was always the same, and days drifted into years with the drinking becoming more and more dominant in our lives. Our drinking became as stylized as Kabuki dancing. We each had a special glass and a special chair, separated by a table which held bound volumes of the National Geographic I brought home from the library where I worked. Every night we would sit, drink, and read about the places we were going to visit "someday." But the reality, of course, was that we never went anywhere. We hid out in our little house with the drapes drawn, as our world got smaller and smaller.

After five years of this life, the university decided not to renew Fran's teaching contract. By this time, he was jaundiced, overweight, with an alcoholic palsy, which made it hard to correct papers. Despite all these symptoms and despite the many days of work I missed because of hangovers, we still did not think there was anything wrong with our drinking. In fact, we thought we were great drinkers! So, it was all the more amazing that one day, with no talk about it in advance, Fran dialed the number of Alcoholics Anonymous in the telephone book. That night, an AA member named Paul came to our door and when he saw us both, he thought, Two for the price of one!

He brought the Big Book and some pamphlets and spent an hour telling us his story. We laughed as we never had before because it was the first time we had ever heard anyone talk honestly about drinking. We were eager to tell him about our lives, but he assured us that he already knew all about our lives. We couldn't understand that remark at the time, but, of course, we know now how sad and pathetic we must have looked that night. After Paul left, we were exuberant, so we finished the fifth of scotch we had hidden in the closet and read the entire Big Book until dawn.

The next day, Paul called and offered to take us to a meeting that night if we would stay sober until then. We agreed, and we went with Paul that night and every night for the next thirty days. He and his loving wife, Louise, absorbed us into their lives. Soon after that, Fran was offered a teaching position at a university in the Pacific Northwest. With six months of sobriety, we packed all our belongings into a small sedan and it all fit, with room to spare for us and our epileptic dog, which should have been some indication to us that after 12 years of marriage, our life had become unmanageable.

The first days of sobriety were difficult because even though our life was miserable in so many ways, it was familiar, while sobriety was unknown territory. We went to meetings early, helped set up, and then after the meetings, we helped clean the ashtrays, replace the chairs— anything to avoid going home. Older members thought we were so dedicated, but the reality was that we had never been together sober, and we didn't know how to relate to one another. We had no idea how to create a sober marriage, and we were too proud to ask for much help. Above all, we found it difficult to make love. Our sexual relationship had been based on scotch, bourbon, and beer—and relating to one another in sobriety was almost embarrassing. We clung to the slogans, "This Too Shall Pass," and "One Day at a Time." And we tried very hard to give one another emotional space. We also tried very hard to live in the present, not dwelling on what our future together might be.

The more we learned about AA, the more dazzled we were. We found the spiritual diversity that we had been seeking all those drinking years. The Steps made perfect sense, and the idea of a "God as I understand him" was crucial to our acceptance. We found the intellectual freedom that always had been so important to us. And everywhere we turned, there were loving and caring AA members who helped us over the rough spots.

The path to recovery was not always smooth. Though neither of us took a drink since that night we first read the AA literature, we struggled through periods of depression and fear. We learned that we each had to build a personal program of recovery. We selected different home groups and, most of the time, attended different meetings. It was important for us to realize that we sometimes "played" to each other at meetings or held something back, thinking of the impact on the other. We took different paths in service and sponsored different people. And although Paul sponsored us both when he was alive, after he died, we each turned to different AA peers for guidance.

As we write this today, we have been married for 47 years—36 of them sober. The blessings which came to us through sobriety include adopting two wonderful children (one sober in AA). Fran received his Ph.D. and eventually retired as a professor emeritus. I, too, retired from a position I loved, and we both have had many opportunities to serve AA. We have an ever-growing American, Canadian, and international group of friends and relatives in AA who care about us. Above all, we have found the true meaning of love and marriage.

In the beginning, it was sometimes difficult to have two sets of alcoholic problems and defects to deal with, but the joy of double sobriety outweighed that. We have learned not to take one another's inventory (even when it is so obvious what would help!), and we've also learned "personal recovery depends upon AA unity." That unity begins at home. We've ceased wondering why all these good things have happened to us and have tried instead to accept them all with grateful hearts—and to pass the gift of AA on.

Jan and Fran P.
Spokane, Washington

A Love Story
May 1998

P eople often ask me how I met my husband of 22 years. I guess it's fairly unusual for people of the "baby boomer" generation to marry young and stay married—happily—for so many years. But how do I tell them?

We met in a bar. There is no disguising this, although people often find this amusing—or ironic, since neither of us has had a drink in 17 years. But Michael and I know the truth. Drinking was the central force, the top priority in our lives at that time, so it's no accident that drinking brought us together.

It was a bar on the Upper East Side of Manhattan. I was drinking to forget the no-good two-timer I was seeing, and Michael had the night off from his much-too-young girlfriend. I first noticed him fiddling with the controls on the bar TV, drinking bourbon on the rocks. I eyed him as he ran through the channels. He was cute enough, I thought. I let him buy me a Manhattan. We talked. I dumped the two-timer, he dumped the jailbait. After a few months, I moved in with him.

In the beginning we had a lot of laughs. We drank "socially," which is to say a drink or two before dinner, wine with, coffee and cognac after. We attended and gave parties regularly. There was always liquor and wine in the house. We fit right in with the lifestyles of almost everyone we knew—witty, urbane, creative people, some with a dusting of celebrity. Everybody we knew drank as much or more than we did. There was nothing to suggest there was anything wrong with our lifestyle.

When we got married after living together for a few years, we had a one-night honeymoon in the Plaza Hotel in New York City. The only people present at our wedding were our two best friends, heavy drinkers like ourselves, who lived next door. They acted as our best man and matron of honor. It was an all-day party, moving from the church in the morning to a giddy dinner at a Polynesian restaurant, where the four of us shared a blue cocktail full of fruit and little boats that came in a glass the size of a basin, to the honeymoon suite at the Plaza for champagne and hilarity until late in the evening. The best man, an amateur movie-maker, decided to direct the story of our wedding night. No, it wasn't like it sounds—it was chaste enough to show at the reception my parents gave for us a few weeks later. In this silent movie, we are very young, very giddy, and very drunk. I don't remember much more of my wedding night except for what was caught on film.

A number of years went by in which Michael's career took off. He worked with top names in the film business, we traveled some, lived in San Francisco for a while, and then, when a lengthy project that had taken us to California was finished, we drove across the country in a covered pickup truck with our cat Sylphie.

But well before we undertook this adventure, there was trouble brewing in our drinking paradise. Though we bent elbows side by side every night, I was more concerned about Michael's drinking than my own. I called the local AA chapter one night and told the nice lady on the phone about this drinking problem my husband had. When she asked me if my own drinking might be cause for even more concern than my husband's, I found her to be impertinent. When she suggested I check out an AA meeting for myself, I quickly hung up the phone.

After that I began to try to control my drinking. I switched from hard stuff to wine, then swore off white wine because it made me "shrill." Then I began counting the calories in my alcohol intake. Nothing really worked; I was simply, as they say, changing seats on the Titanic.

By the time we left on our cross-country trip, I made a vow to Michael that I wouldn't drink until we reached New York. When he seemed unimpressed, I asked him to swear off with me. He agreed, but I knew in my heart he wasn't committed—the spineless weakling, I thought with contempt. So when he poured himself a whiskey the second night out, I angrily opened a bottle of cheap wine and told him how we'd failed our experiment and it was all his fault.

One day in late spring, after we'd been back in New York for about five months, I was talking to a friend of mine about trying to cut back on my drinking. Drinking, to my mind, was merely a "calorie" problem. I was trying to lose weight, and everyone knows drinking is a culprit. I told her I must be doing something right, because I seemed, over the previous few weeks, to have suddenly lost my taste for alcohol. It even made me nauseous at times. She looked at me strangely. "The only time I ever lost my taste for alcohol," said this mother of two, "was when I was pregnant." Her words caused me to stop dead in my tracks.

I hadn't expected or planned to become pregnant, but a few days later it was confirmed: baby due in December.

What followed over those next few months is hard to describe. I don't believe there were ever two people less prepared to open their lives to a new baby. Instead of reading, talking to other parents, attending classes, we both dwelled in fantasy: I would take the baby with me in a backpack when I had interviews or other writing assignments; he or she would play quietly at my feet while I wrote in the afternoons. Michael was heard to say that having the baby was the very thing he needed to help him grow up and straighten out his life.

Though it seems incredible now, in 1980 there was little known about the effects of drinking on pregnancy. When my "taste for alcohol" returned, my obstetrician told me I could have two drinks a day. And I did. Every day.

The months crept by. One night in October, at dinner at a friend's house, I went over my two-drink limit. As I kept filling my glass, I wondered when someone was going to stop me, because I couldn't stop myself. The next morning, filled with remorse, I noticed the baby moving sluggishly. I prayed that everything would be all right, and swore that I'd never get drunk again.

But a month later I did, and in the middle of a nasty fight with Michael, who was also drunk, I suddenly stopped. Something felt wrong. I was very still within myself, and the stillness seemed to go on and on. I turned a listening ear to the baby inside me and I went to bed. I was still listening the next morning as I arose, feeling for movement that didn't come. That night I was admitted to the hospital, and an ultrasound confirmed that the baby was dead.

Birthing our baby daughter, after the doctor had induced labor that December day, was a nightmare. Even with Michael at my side, I felt like I was at the bottom of a well. I didn't cry when she finally tumbled out, but Michael, swept with sobs, buried his face in my shoulder. I would feel that way later, but at the time all I felt was an eerie calm, and the thought came to me: She gave her life for something; I have to find out what it is.

A few weeks later, a friend offered us the use of a cabin in Vermont where we could escape the holiday season bearing down on us. A coworker of Michael's had given us some AA literature, which I'd thrown in the overnight bag with some magazines and books. In between raiding the liquor cabinet, I read through the literature and found out to my utter astonishment that I qualified as an alcoholic.

Wait a minute! I didn't hide bottles in flowerpots, drink in the morning, or fail to show up for work, so how could I be an alcoholic?

Michael had started going to AA meetings, and after a while I did too. The months went by like those fast-forward movie calendar pages, yet each day crawled. I took all of my feelings to meetings, and little by little, I started to get better. Still, my husband was all but a stranger to me.

During that first year of sobriety, he worked long hours while I drifted aimlessly, taking odd jobs here and there. My emotions were on a roller-coaster, and I didn't know whether that was due to stopping drinking or grieving the loss of our baby. My main focus was going to meetings, and waiting.

I was waiting until I could get pregnant again—that was the only thing I wanted. And yet in AA rooms I kept hearing that I shouldn't make any major changes during the first year. I was convinced that if I didn't get well and truly sober—which meant doing as I was told in AA—I would never have a healthy baby. I followed the suggestion.

A year and a month after we lost our daughter, the seed of our new baby—and the seed of an entirely new us—began to stir. The new pregnancy was light years away from the first. We chose a midwife (so I could make it through childbirth drug-free), I drank herbal concoctions instead of alcoholic ones, and I gave up the only things I still indulged in—tea and diet soda.

At last he arrived: our firstborn son. He was robust and striking, and I congratulated myself on two years of sober living. But the kid was a love sponge! Neither Michael nor I had ever before experienced loving someone so completely. It was exhilarating. We fawned over him. He was a wonder.

The only question was: who was this *other* person—the one each of us was married to?

We had come to the next hurdle in our long haul: pulling our heads down out of the clouds of love for this miracle we'd created, and refocusing on ourselves and our relationship. We had to start dating again. It was awkward at first; we had trouble thinking of things to say. Sometimes we'd just go to a meeting together. Gradually, we found each other again.

Drinking may have brought us together, but we discovered much more about each other that we both valued, like raising children without fear or violence of word or deed. We also discovered a strong spiritual core in AA that fitted both of us perfectly, and it bound us together in a way that alcohol, our old god, once had.

As anyone who gets sober or lives with someone in sobriety knows,

AA doesn't make perfect people out of us. In fact, there's possibly more work to do in the care and feeding of a dual-sober relationship, because recovery might not happen at the same rate of speed. Over the years we had some terrible arguments, and at times it almost seemed as if we might never bridge the gulf that could open up over incidents great and small. But whenever these breakdowns occurred, we each had only one real way of dealing with it—the AA program.

Fortunately, that was enough to start. During the times when we could barely be civil, speaking to each other in chilly tones about the grocery list or the kids' school bus schedules, we could still manage to strike a spark of warmth by sharing an insight from a meeting or a sponsor call. From there, we might find common ground, and even acceptance. Sooner or later, one or both of us would be on our way to a meeting, offering grudging amends later.

We still go to meetings together, and have brought each of our three children as infants into the meeting rooms of AA, to be cuddled and watched over by our sober friends while we listened to much-needed experience, strength, and hope. We have raised our children to understand that, statistically speaking, they have a pretty fair chance of becoming addicted to alcohol. We have told them parts of our story and encouraged them to ask questions. We have shared with them our concept of a Higher Power, and some of the AA slogans have served well as family mottoes.

A former drinking buddy once remarked, as he reminisced about the old days, that our fast crowd had been made up of some very special people, people of extremes: big hearts, big egos, big risks, and big falls. The people dear to us now are equally unique and remarkable, but for their wisdom, their healthy outlook, and for the look in their eyes that says they have been down hard roads in life, and survived.

If two people are destined to be together, then I believe that they will triumph over all that comes their way. I also believe that this kind of couple proves the theory of the whole being greater than the sum of its parts. I believe my husband Michael and I were destined to be together, and that God had it in mind that our little lost child would be the instrument whereby our feet could be planted on the road to becoming a greater whole. We thank God every day that AA was the destination and the journey on that road we began together so many years ago.

Donna M.
Ossining, New York

Sobriety and Divorce
October 1977

S peaking at an AA convention, I told about the good and bad things that have happened to me over the 18 years I've enjoyed continuous sobriety. I tried to communicate to the audience that when we're sober, both desirable and undesirable things happen to us, just as they do to other human beings. The fact that we get sober doesn't mean that bad experiences or unpleasant events will never occur in our lives.

Without going into any great detail, I used this as an example: After my 18 years of sobriety, some irreconcilable differences arose between my wife and me. We were divorced, after 21 years of marriage. As bad as the experience was, and no matter how much it hurt, the Fellowship of AA made it possible for me to go through that whole time without drinking.

It was amazing how many people approached me after that talk and over the next two days of the convention, commenting on divorce in sobriety. Many people said that they were faced with the same situation, but that it remained unresolved and was a constant source of inner warfare. Several said they had gotten drunk as a result.

Some typical reasons for not resolving the situation were: What would people think? How can I divorce my spouse? After all, he (she) stayed with me when I was drinking. I just couldn't go through a divorce. And there were many more. The point is, quite a few people continued in their unresolved dilemma, and periodically they drank. For us, to drink is often to die.

Divorce is a touchy subject, and it is very difficult to terminate a marriage after 21 years. It's like experiencing the death of a loved one. We must deal with anger, a great sense of loss, and an almost overwhelming sense of aloneness and separation. But all these are feelings that human beings can cope with. Alcoholics are human, and if we are working the program and attending meetings (rather than sitting around and feeling sorry for ourselves), we don't have to take that first and often fatal drink.

When asked for advice or counsel on divorce in sobriety, I try to explain that I can't make decisions for other people. How can I possibly tell you whether to stay married or get a divorce? I can't play God. What I can do is refer you to that old AA tool, the Serenity Prayer. "God grant me the serenity to accept the things I cannot change, courage to change the things I can, and wisdom to know the difference."

If we apply this prayer to a troubled marriage, we must either accept the marriage as it is or change it. One of the ways of changing it—the most radical, to be sure—is divorce. It is painful and unpleasant, but it's not something to get drunk over. We can endure, tolerate, accept, and recover.

No matter how difficult divorce may be, it is a fact of life even for people with fairly long periods of sobriety. After almost a year of living in an apartment alone, I can say that because of the Fellowship of AA, I am alive and healthy and still sober. I am living well and enjoying the benefits the AA way of life offers when we pray for the courage to know the difference between what we can accept and what we must change.

L. R.
Lexington, Kentucky

Marriage
March 1980

E
arly on in my AA life, I was truly grateful for the chance the Fellowship was giving me for sobriety. But I didn't really think it would work for me, because I didn't believe in God—or anything else, for that matter.

Around other AAs and at meetings, I felt reasonably well, but as soon as I walked through the door of my home, I returned to the monster-like behavior I had displayed during my 20 years of alcoholic drinking. I hated myself, and this feeling confused me and frustrated me.

During those first two years sober, I announced to my sponsor that I didn't know if I loved my wife. I said I wanted to, but just didn't know if I could. My sponsor, bless him, told me to act *as if* I did. I fought his logic, answering, "That's dishonest, and AA demands total honesty. I can't do it."

Near the end of my second AA year, my lovely wife agreed to a divorce. She just couldn't go on with the doubts and fears she must have had. I felt that this was the answer for me and that I would now become happy and have the true serenity that I had heard you folks talk about.

When I look back on it now, I know that the only person I cared about was me. The fact that my wife really loved me and that we had five children didn't concern me. "Act as if," indeed! My sponsor was a very wise person, but he goofed that time, I thought.

Well, we separated, and during the month I lived alone in an apartment, I found the true meaning of the message my sponsor was giving me. Filled with self-pity, I turned to God, *acting as if* I believed in him. I asked for the wisdom to learn the truth. The truth I sought turned out to be this: For 38 years, I had been negative and selfish. To laugh, to feel happy, to love someone were all strange to me, and until I was willing to let happiness in, I could not change.

My wife and I renewed our wedding vows two years ago. I truly love her, and I truly love life. She has Al-Anon, and she says she probably would never have found her happiness without it, just as I could not have found mine without AA.

I could always picture the person I wanted to be—loving, kind, gentle, understanding, and happy. But until I began to practice being that person, I remained the same miserable grouch, filled with confusion and self-pity. I owe AA my life.

J. L.

Hatteras, North Carolina

Just Friends
May 2010

One of the many gifts I have received in my almost 12 years of sobriety is the work I was allowed to do at a local transition home for recovering alcoholics and addicts. I guess I just have a way with drunks, because I am one.

One of my favorite topics is one that involves relationships in recovery. At least once a week, someone would come home and want to tell us about the girl he met in detox or at a meeting. As the "Twelve and Twelve" says: "boy meets girl on AA campus and love follows at first sight." Of course when I questioned them about such things, I always got the same response. "Oh it's not like that. We're just friends." And I would always say the same thing: "Let me tell you a story about that."

In addition to being a member of AA, I am also a grateful member of Al-Anon. It's ironic. I originally went to Al-Anon because I thought it would be a great place to meet women who knew how to take care of alcoholics. But, when I heard the members, both male and female, talk about their experiences, how they were affected by the alcoholism of others and how they found solutions, well, I realized I belonged there too. So, I would always go to one Al-Anon meeting a week, a 10 A.M. early bird meeting. The rest of the week I spent in AA.

Well! There was this one lady who was always at the meeting. She always looked really stressed out, to the point of exhaustion, head down, eyes closed. I thought she came to the meetings to sleep somewhere she knew she'd be safe. I later learned that she wasn't sleeping, she was meditating. Every now and then, she would laugh and whenever she did—no word of lie—everything around her got brighter. When she shared, her voice was soft and soothing. Sometimes I went to that meeting just to hear her laugh. She was a very nice lady, very spiritual. Her name was Nancy, which means "full of grace." I was attracted to her but not in the man-woman kind of way. It was deeper, more of a spiritual attraction. But I stayed clear of women in Al-Anon because I was still new in sobriety, and I felt they had probably suffered enough without having to put up with me, too.

Life is seldom so uncomplicated. One day, she spoke to me outside a meeting. She asked me for a light. I asked her for a cigarette. We exchanged small talk about the weather. It was nothing out of the ordinary. At the time, I had been sober about four months and I was living in the same transition home where I later went to work. The following Monday I was late getting to the meeting. I wasn't even going to go. I get a weird feeling every time I think what might have happened if I hadn't gone. The meeting was almost over. The topic was the slogans, I think. I shared about a slogan an AA friend had recently told me about. "If you want something you never had before, then do something you never did before." I thought it sounded cool.

After the meeting, Nancy cornered me and said she was going to do something she'd never done before. She asked me if I would tell her what it was like to be an alcoholic because her husband (with whom she was going through a messy divorce) had never talked about it to her. I suggested she go to an open AA speaker meeting. By coincidence, there was one that night, so I gave her the location. She asked if I was planning to attend, and I said I was and if she was nervous she could certainly sit in my row. She offered to drive me there, and I thought that was a great idea. It was all very platonic and harmless because, after all, we were "just friends" and I was just being helpful.

The meeting was at 8; she picked me up at 6. Some of the guys were razzing me about it. I assured them it wasn't what they were thinking. "It's not like that. We're just friends." The interesting part is that we were just friends. We had a few hours to kill so we went for coffee, shared some polite conversation and some kidding around. I told her what the guys had said and she laughed. There it was again. I felt very relaxed in her presence. One of us made a comment that we should get to the meeting because this was starting to feel like a date, but it wasn't a date. Was it?

The meeting was great. The place was packed. The speaker was powerful. There was lots of laughter, lots of tears and lots of love. Nancy was floored by the whole thing. Afterward she remarked that she felt like she had been hit in the stomach with a 2x4. She didn't know whether to laugh, cry or throw up. The meeting was over at 9. Since we were having such a great time, we decided to have another coffee and take a drive along the coast. OK, so maybe that part was a bit romantic, but it was her idea.

Nancy and I had similar stories. We had grown up in the same neighborhoods, we knew a lot of the same people, we drank in the same places, we felt the same feelings, we liked a lot of the same types of food and the same music, we both liked dancing—I'd never realized how much in common we actually had. I'd never really taken the time to get to know her; I was afraid of screwing it up. As her story unfolded, something happened. I realized that I was in love with Nancy. I figured I had probably been in love with her since the day I laid eyes on her and that no matter what happened next, I would always be in love with her. So, I kissed her. I figured this could go two ways. Either she would kiss me back or she would throw me out of her truck. Well, obviously she didn't throw me out of her truck.

The following day, Nancy and I went to a noon meeting. Afterward, I told her why I kissed her and after I got up from being down on one knee, we decided we would walk this road together. My sponsor wasn't crazy about the idea but he liked the fact that I was on Step Nine when I proposed, and not Step One. I truly believe that was why we were so successful in what we set out to do. We had solid programs. Our "compatibility at spiritual, mental and emotional levels [was] a fact and not wishful thinking," as it says in the essay on Step Twelve in the "Twelve and Twelve." To further paraphrase the essay, we were as sure as possible that no deep-lying emotional handicaps would rise up under later pressures to cripple us.

I've always believed that without AA, I'd have nothing and I'd be nothing, so my program takes precedence over everything else. Nancy later became a member of our Fellowship and will celebrate 12 years in September.

I also said that it would be nice if I could promise Nancy the moon and the stars and that I would love her until the end of time, but I didn't know what I would be doing at the end of time—all I could offer her was one day, today. That was March 24, 1998. One day at a time has been working just fine. We were married on New Years Eve, 1999. I sent everyone an invitation. It was in the December 1999 Grapevine: "Invitation to a Wedding." Some of you even showed up.

Someone once said that the relationship the two of us have is remarkable. She wanted to know what our secret was. She even said we should put it in a bottle and sell it. We just laughed because it's no secret really. If you take the Twelve Steps, the Twelve Traditions and the Twelve Concepts, and apply them to your life on a daily basis, you will be amazed at the results you get. No need to put it in a bottle. It's already in a book. It's called *Alcoholics Anonymous* and it not only saved our lives, it gave us new life. And by the way, we're still friends.

Bernie S.
Dartmouth, Nova Scotia

Let's Get a Divorce!
January 1977

So I made one year, and they *weren't* lying! Everything was better, just like they said it would be in meeting after meeting. Some of the fear dropped away, the paranoia—I could actually see a cop without having my bowels contract—and I figured if I made another year, I'd try getting involved with the human race again, maybe try answering the phone, going out into the yard. That sort of thing. (I mean, I was sick!)

After the year, I slid for another six months, making meetings, getting cocky, and it was right about then—with a year and six months—that I decided to get a divorce.

Just like that. No reason. I have a beautiful wife. She loves me and I love her. She stuck by me through some stuff that ... well, we all know about those days, don't we?

But I decided to get a divorce, decided to make a change. I was sober, so why didn't I just go ahead and fix my whole life up and make it *all* new? (At least, I think that's what I was thinking—if I was thinking at all.)

My wife was surprisingly pleasant. "You're out of your gourd," she said, smiling not unkindly. The same smile she'd used when I rediscovered sex, came home with a 160-pound Great Dane and 26 chickens, learned to practice scream therapy, and bought a six-foot plant that I named Igor—all of which decisive actions were part of my recovery process. She gave me that same smile. "You wouldn't last 20 minutes without me."

"Seriously," I said. "I think we should split the blanket. We're living together because of the drunk thing." (I'd met her during my drinking days.) "We should try it another way sober."

For a long time, she studied me—about the way a cobra looks at a bird just before striking. "There's nobody else, is there?"

"Well, no. Raquel Welch, maybe, but other than that, no." I shook my head. "And I don't think she's available."

"So what's all this about a divorce?" Again the sharp look. "Don't you love me?"

I nodded. "Yup. More than ever. I just think we should make sure we aren't staying married because of the drunk thing."

Well, hell, nobody says you have to be smart to be a drunk, right? So I went right ahead and talked myself into a pit—just like in the old days. When I got done, she gave me That Look again, smiled, and said, "All right. Let's try an experiment. We'll stay in the same house—to save money—but we won't talk, won't do *anything* with each other. Just like we were divorced. All right?"

For the record: I made more than 20 minutes. She was wrong there. I made a lot more than a mere 20 minutes. I made it almost a full day. There are parts of that day I'd like to forget, because I don't think it's good for your sobriety to dwell on things that are unpleasant.

That night for supper, for instance, I ate a television dinner that was made in 1943. By the Germans. In revenge. (How do they get the potatoes like that?)

Then I went down to wash clothes in a washer designed by a maniac. I swear the damn thing growled at me, and it was just a miracle that I got out of the basement alive—it jumped at me during the spin cycle.

But the worst thing was all that stuff that happened during the day that I wanted to *talk* to somebody about—not just anybody, but a Program Person. I mean, we're different, and seemingly ordinary things are different for us. Like, a flat tire to a nonalcoholic is just that, a flat tire; a flat tire to a drunk can mean anything from the air leaking out of the tire to a major change in life structure and philosophical leanings, depending on the moon, the phase of sobriety, and whether or not the spare is also flat.

Things would happen like that, and I'd turn to tell my wife, my Al-Anon, the one who'd ridden the river with me. And now I couldn't *talk* to her.

That was the worst. Not having that other Program Person around, the other person who would *understand*, and the more I thought about it, the more I realized that she was right. I was out of my gourd.

I cracked about 11 that night. I'd been working on the tire (yes, the spare was flat, too, and I'd spent all day just getting a goddamn tire changed), and I finally got the thing fixed, and I rushed in the house, and there she sat, with that same smile on her face, and I looked at her for a full minute, the whole day's steam building up in me ...

"The hell with it!" I cried. And I glommed onto a cup of coffee and sat down across the table from her. "See, it was like this. The tire was flat and the spare was down too, and I had to get the spare fixed, then run the regular tire over to get that fixed, and I didn't drink ..."

Of course, I talked to my sponsor later, and he told me that I'd simply gone through the Great Big Divorce Hassle—apparently common with recovering drunks who decide they should remake their whole lives to conform to the bliss of their newfound sobriety. Everybody does it.

But revenge is sweet, nonetheless. Al-Anons always win, of course, but this time I got at least a little even. I made her sit all night listening to me tell her about my day—the washer, the television dinner, the tire. All of it.

And I didn't even notice the smile.

G. P.

Elbert, Colorado

Love Story
November 1958

Although I am not an alcoholic, I am one of the many people who have benefited indirectly, but no less greatly, by the program of Alcoholics Anonymous.

My story is basically a love story, though I want to confess that I am a most improbable subject for a tale of romance. I am a 34-year-old housewife and the mother of six children.

Ridiculous as it may seem, coming from a person like me, in the past few months I have fallen breathtakingly, head-over-heels in love, for the first and only time. Oddly enough, I have AA to thank for the wonderful new emotion that has come into my life.

He is someone I met only a few months ago, this man I love. He is wonderful, strong, dependable, considerate. He has all the fine qualities I envied more fortunate women in their mates, during the long painful years when I was married to a man who couldn't control his drinking. Other AA wives will recognize immediately the identity of the wonderful new man who has come into my life. He is the man my husband has become since joining AA.

Nothing I can say is not well known to any woman who has been the wife of a problem drinker, but perhaps there will be something in my experience that will help to clarify for some puzzled husband, new in AA membership, the riddle of why the little woman reacted as she did—first to the problem of his out-of-control drinking and later to the changes which a husband's participation in AA make in a marriage relationship.

Unfortunately, I never knew my husband before alcohol became a dominant factor in his life. If I had, perhaps this new personality of his would not have come as such a surprise to me. I realize now that it is not really a new personality at all. It was there all the time but so obscured by habits of alcoholic thinking and alcoholic behavior that even I, who should have known him best, really didn't know him at all. I mistook the lies, the vacillation, the selfishness, the petty deceits and the lack of self-confidence—part of the pattern of alcoholism—for an intrinsic part of my husband's character and personality. I have since learned that they were only symptoms of his illness—no more a part of the real man than the slurred speech and stumbling gait of drunkenness.

For years I considered myself the strong one in our marriage. I, alone, made any effort to pay our mountain of bills, to give our children the little stability they received, to hold together our shaky marriage and increasingly unhappy home. I was a victim of my own over-inflated ego. I saw myself as a heroic little martyr, struggling alone to carry the burden of responsibility for my family. I would have scoffed at the notion that, in the drunken weakling I considered my husband to be, I would find a strong ally, a person far better qualified than I to lead our family to a better, richer life. Humility, a word I have often heard at the open meetings I have attended with my husband, had little real meaning for me before AA came into our lives.

I knew in a vague way that I had some faults. Hadn't everyone? I was a very indifferent housekeeper, but wasn't that justified by the fact that my husband's drinking had lost us the house we were buying and necessitated our moving through a procession of progressively shabbier rented houses that never seemed like home?

I made little effort to dress attractively but wasn't that excusable since my husband's drinking left little money for clothes or makeup? Surely displays of bad temper, nagging, sarcasm and spells of sulkiness could be forgiven to a woman who lived under the strain of being married to a problem drinker.

In short, just as my husband used alcohol as a crutch, I used my husband's alcoholism as a crutch to explain away my faults and justify my own shortcomings. I didn't drive my husband to drink. He drank excessively and abnormally for some years before he met me. But instead of dealing constructively with my own problems, I placed the burden of my own failures on top of the burden which my husband already carried—the illness of alcoholism.

I don't pretend to know much about alcoholism. I do know that just as I cannot blame myself for causing my husband's illness neither can I accept any of the credit for his new freedom from the compulsion to drink. It is true that I am trying harder than I ever tried before to be a good wife and to make my husband happy, but even I am not foolish enough to delude myself that any effort on my part could keep my husband from drinking. He is sober because he wants to be sober, because in AA he has found a new way of life in which he is happier than he was in the old one.

I urged my husband to join AA, naively believing that with AA to reform him he might become worthy of his children and of me. What colossal conceit! Since that day I have had to adjust my thinking tremendously. It is I who must work hard and continuously to be worthy of the wonderful man to whom I am married.

He has had one slip. After attending AA meetings for a couple of months he decided to experiment one day to see if he could take one or two drinks and stop. The result was inevitable, but it left him even more determined than ever to make the AA program work for him.

I have had hundreds of slips, slips into arrogance, conceit, wrong thinking, but with God's help it always comes right again. My husband isn't alone in AA. We are an AA family. We try to live and think and work with the AA Steps and Traditions in mind. One doesn't have to have been a problem drinker to benefit from the wisdom of living one day at a time or to place one's trust in a power greater than ourselves.

That is one bond which you as alcoholics and we who are non-alcoholics have in common. As human beings we are all subject to the same foolish vanities, to patterns of wrong thinking and immature behavior. We can all benefit from taking stock of ourselves and taking constructive steps to build our lives into something better and richer for our own sakes and for those who are dear to us.

I cannot say that I am glad that my husband is an alcoholic for he has suffered more than so fine a person should ever have to suffer. I am glad, though, that I have been given an opportunity to become acquainted with the AA program and have found for myself and my family a better way of life through Alcoholics Anonymous.

J. G. D.
Saugerties, New York

Finding Love Again on AA Campus
Grapevine Online Exclusive – March 2011

was six months short of 40 when I took my last drink. My two children were in junior high and high school, driving me crazy, and I had a marriage that was in the final stages of destruction. I learned in my sobriety that my drinking was the primary cause of the misery in my life although I didn't think so. I was very angry to learn from the winners that I was not to make any major changes in relationships the first year of my sobriety because I wanted a divorce, and that would solve most of my problems. But I wanted what you had and I listened and followed the advice. My attitude changed and by my first AA birthday I sincerely wanted to save my marriage and make it work. It was not to be, there was way too much baggage of the past that kept being blown back to my side of the street, and I didn't have a willing partner who would work on her side. I moved out, and a few weeks later, the divorce papers were served. A marriage of almost 23 years was over, due to my drinking.

I was finished with women—they were a source of misery. I decided to stay a bachelor for the rest of my life. I wanted nothing to do with any other women. I would now be able to hunt, fish and do what I wanted, when I wanted, without anyone's permission. As usual, my intentions were no prediction of my future. I continued with my program and went to a lot of meetings. I joined in with others for coffee or ice cream and occasionally lunch or dinner. I learned how to interact with others without having an agenda. I also started listening closer to people, especially those who shared regularly about their Higher Power. I was attracted to the women who shared their Higher Power. I started thinking that spiritual women were the most beautiful people on earth. After a time, the group after the meeting was getting smaller when we would go out. Then one night it got down to just two of us. The other person was this lady who was very open and honest about her God. The fact that she was pretty and had a nice figure was a plus. I think we just went for coffee after that meeting.

Not long after that night I was in my new apartment doing laundry when the phone rang and it was her. She had an extra ticket for a play and invited me to go with her. I valued her friendship so I accepted. At this point in my life I needed a good laugh and we laughed all through the play and afterward when we went to eat. That was the start of being running buddies that developed into friendship.

I had learned and been told that unless I could determine my part in past relationships, I would be condemned to repeat my mistakes. I learned that drunks have a picker that is broken and when it comes to the opposite sex, we will pick someone who fits our old ideas of what the ideal partner should be. And as we know—the results are nil until we let go absolutely.

The first paragraph in Step Eight in the "Twelve and Twelve" tells us we are to examine our relationships. The first full paragraph on page 80 speaks volumes about what we are to do. We are to find those flaws which are basic and responsible for the whole pattern of our lives. This is an expanded version of the inventory we took in Step Four. I added this to another Fifth Step and in the Sixth and Seventh Steps asked God to remove the character defects which I used to sabotage and destroy every relationship I had in the past. As I became willing to change my behavior and God removed my defects of character that pertained to relationships, I was able to maintain a healthy relationship and make it grow. I was the beneficiary of the promise at the end of the paragraph: "Thoroughness, we have found, will pay—and pay handsomely."

I say all of this because in the course of becoming a running buddy and a friend, I was starting to fall in love again. I didn't want it, I didn't think it was possible and I knew I was no good in the field of love. Without knowing it, I had surrendered once more. I was learning how to love others unconditionally just as my Higher Power loved me. I was learning how to be a friend, I was keeping promises, I was a sympathetic listener, and I was considering others before I was thinking of myself. I was changing and learning how to be a man and a partner.

Many months went by as we spent more and more time together. I met her family and could see she was from good stock. My family came to visit, and during the course of the visit, we shared a big meal at her folks' home. I was sitting next to my aunt and I asked her a question: "Does this setting remind you of anything?" Her answer was, "Reminds me of our family back home." I felt the same thing. It was something I had been missing for a long time. My ex-wife and I had lived so far apart from our families; we missed a lot of holidays, birthdays and anniversaries. I felt very at home in my new lady friend's family. I was accepted and I felt loved.

No discussion of dating in sobriety would be complete unless it included intimacy. Being intimate is not about sex. I learned that intimacy is sharing from the heart without being judged. It is based on trust. For many years I confused intimacy with sex. Sex is biology and hormones with a lot of emotional baggage. My new lady friend and I had progressed over a period of months from shaking hands and a hug at the end of the evening to a kiss on the cheek. Finally one night we shared a real kiss and it was both electric and frightening. My first thought was, My God, what have I done? I have ruined everything now. Over the next few weeks we both did something different—we talked about our feelings concerning the first kiss and the hormones we had brought back to life. We knew the logical conclusion but were afraid sex would ruin a good friendship. We decided to pray about it and ask our Higher Power to guide us in this new and unfamiliar territory. We followed his path and we haven't looked back.

What I learned about my part in old relationships I decided to do differently in my new life in recovery. I let God choose and it has worked out extremely well. I also learned and adopted a new set of beliefs.

1. If I can't love myself, I am incapable of loving another. The program of recovery has allowed me to get to know me and to love myself.

2. Love God and follow his plan for me. I am not always certain of the next right thing to do, but I always know the wrong thing to do so I do not practice my old behavior.

3. Love others as I would love myself.

The result has been 14 years in a happy marriage and more than 20 years of sobriety. We respect and cherish each other, we have learned how to resolve conflicts, and by working our programs, we continue to take inventory and make amends as needed. We have been through times of unemployment, health issues, burying both of our fathers and life situations in general. We let God be in charge and things work out.

We went into this relationship knowing that when boy meets girl on AA turf, the results are not always good. After all, we are people who normally would not mix. We also have to remember that as recovering alcoholics, we bring a lot of baggage into a relationship, and a lot of us are not a real catch. We have issues! But experience has taught us that if we put God in charge and practice these principles in all our affairs, all things are possible. Thanks be to God.

Robert M.
Carrollton, Texas

―――――――――――――――――――――――――

A Square
April 1960

once heard an AA speaker say, "If you pray for something, look out! You might get it." He explained that an answer to prayer, in the guise of great good fortune, can be a calamity to someone who is not mentally and emotionally prepared for new responsibilities.

Two years ago I married "the most wonderful man in the world," another AA. This was the answer to my prayers, for I had prayed to be happily married to a man who would be happy with me. Our marriage followed a whirlwind courtship; we hardly knew one another. We had a beautiful wedding on a June day. We left the ceremony knowing that a power greater than ourselves had brought us together.

We are not in our first youth. My husband was a bachelor; I had been married twice before, one marriage inspired by alcohol. I now thought of myself as a mature, secure, disciplined person. True, compared to my old drunken self, I am St. Theresa and Marilyn Monroe combined. In 10 years I had made progress. But was it enough? I did not look beyond the golden ring on my finger. I was trying to prove something: that I was lovable and desirable, a woman who had got a man. I forgot that this man had got himself a woman. And that this woman was meant to serve in the mature capacity of a wife.

Now I was returning to Philadelphia, the place I had run away from 10 years ago. True, I had come back here to make AA talks. I thought I had made my peace with the old town. The older members of the family are now deceased, and the home of my childhood is in other hands. But when I returned, the old memories revived: the drunken quarrels with my family; the final break, when I walked out on them. Passing that old Victorian red brick structure, I did not turn my head away, I glared at it: "I dare you to intimidate me!" And there were other memories concerning former friends of my youth whom I had hurt and shocked by raising a whole lot of un-merry hell, in ways too numerous to mention and too imaginative to describe.

But here in Philadelphia, Dick has his roots, his family ties, his means of livelihood. But even Dick didn't want to live in his old surroundings. So, just as impulsively as we had gotten married, we got a house. We saw it one day and bought it the next. It's a lovely house in an old run-down neighborhood that's being restored.

Forty-eight hours later, I regretted buying the house. I began to wonder about our marriage. Here we were, renovating a house over our heads! The plaster was falling, the buzz-saw started shrieking at 7 A.M. The carpenter turned out to be a fellow sufferer, unreclaimed. One day he arrived and put in a screen door we hadn't ordered. He had confused us with another client. He kept wandering off the job, as did the painters and the plumbers who installed a new furnace.

The house was a mess for months, and so was I. I wanted to run back home. Dick was not the wise, kind father-mother who would replace a host of dear old AA friends in Cincinnati to whom I could run in any crisis. I missed my doctor, my lawyer, the friendly grocer who delivered, the doorman, the girl at the apartment switchboard, and my landlord, who fixed everything that broke. I was a helpless, spoiled darling, who had suddenly been set on her own. Why hadn't Dick seen to it that we got the right house?

I got into a nervous downward spiral—the good old fear, depression, self-pity routine, that spells danger for the alcoholic.

Dick said, "But I'm a husband, not a father." He dragged me to meetings. AA in Philadelphia was new and strange to me, but being an out-of-towner, I was often asked to speak. Once I absent-mindedly introduced myself by my maiden name, and gave a grand talk, without so much as mentioning Dick. "You gave a good but rather unusual talk," somebody said.

I stayed sober. So did Dick. He is a dedicated AA. "There's nothing bothering you that AA can't straighten out," said he, saying it several times, and patiently.

Finally the house was settled, but I was not. I had not yet found a permanent maid. The nearest grocery store was a second-rate chain store, quite a walking distance, and Dick had to have the car. I had forgotten that cooking a beautiful gourmet meal for an occasional boy friend is very different from getting dinner every night for a full-time man. I had to put out the garbage cans in the stink of gathered trash in a back alley in August. One night a rat ran over my foot.

Everything was wrong and it was Dick's fault. If he had merely been an AA friend, I would have been full of wisdom, love and compassion. I would have understood his own difficulties. But I made his problems into shortcomings and took his inventory every day.

Ah, the sweet old life of Cincinnati, my old, comfortable, protected half-alive life! Where I had been so independent, and yet so helplessly dependent. And where there was no one toward whom I had any continuous responsibility. I said to myself: "You'd like to be back there. And yet you wouldn't. What do you want?"

"I don't want to be any place. I want to get drunk."

"Now, that's dangerous thinking. You know that?"

Yes, I knew that. I considered throwing myself on the bed and having a good cry. But the doorbell rang. It was the plumber. "What seems to be the trouble?" he asked me.

"Something leaks."

"Where?"

"I don't know. Yesterday, it seems to me, I noticed a leak someplace. Just go over the house and check everything."

I kept on saying my prayers, sometimes hourly. We kept on going to meetings. I had thought that this marriage was the answer to prayer, and Dick had thought so. Now he had that tightly held-in look on his face. I absolutely loathe a nagging spouse. Had I become one of them? But I was only trying to employ the honesty part of the program, wasn't I?

Needless to say, Dick was also on his knees, asking God. Like the blue sky, breaking through clouds, good things began to happen. One by one, my childhood acquaintances welcomed me back to Philadelphia. They all liked Dick, they were interested in AA. We began to make new friends in the neighborhood, other brave souls who were pioneering. The awful hours of sitting around in the silent house were over. An old friend made me go through the family house. She had access to it, and we made a tour of the rooms. I thanked her, and since then, when I pass the elaborate and hideously ornate brick facade, I slip it a friendly wink.

But the plumber sent his bill on the very day that Dick had had a trying time at the office. "It's for $25," he said. "What did we have, a flood? Or a drought?"

"A thorough check," I said.

It happened that I, too, had had a trying day at the chain store. I had gotten a flareup of emotional insecurity over that wire baby carriage you push around. I had tried to push it past the checking counter, and then my packages had gotten mixed up. A line of harassed customers had stared at me. The checker had said, "You have to go back and get these unmarked items weighed." It had taken almost an hour.

"I am not a trained plumber's assistant," I told Dick. "I simply cannot be expected to ..." I went into what I couldn't be expected to do, and Dick listened with a flushed face. Lately his temper had gotten short. He was getting increasingly uncooperative about having his inventory taken. So I took it again, going over old ground, and adding a few new things. It ran about 10 minutes, like a good AA talk.

When I got through, I observed that his face had grown stormy. "I am sick of having the rug pulled out from under me. Every time I need love and understanding, I get hostility and criticism." What was there left for me to say? Nothing, but I said it!

"You're a six foot, rotten, spoiled, immature, unhousebroken alligator," I told him.

He rose from the sofa, walked out into the hall, reached for his hat, and announced, "You're not a wife, you're a reign of terror."

"You're going? But you haven't had your dinner."

"I'll get it elsewhere." The door slammed.

I was furious, I was gleeful. I thought, *good!* Dinner alone at last.

Peace and quiet. I shall enjoy a delicious meal, read a book. I don't care if he ever comes back. But instead I ran upstairs, threw myself on the bed and had that cry I'd been planning on so long. Suppose he doesn't come home?

Suppose he gets drunk?

I went to the telephone and dialed the number of a wise and wonderful AA friend. As I sat waiting for her, I realized that this scene was familiar. In the past, I had so often become upset by things, and let myself become involved in a crisis. I would neglect the business of living, and spend hours and days alternately complaining to patient AAs and brooding alone. I took everything that happened as a personal affront. How often had I not sat thus, waiting for an emergency session with some friend? Yes, I was ready to listen to others. I was an expert in the "what the matter is now" department. I knew I had helped people. But this constant calling for help is selfish. There are other things in life. Just living it, for instance, and living your marriage.

When my friend arrived and I had poured the coffee she said, "I think you're doing fine. Just keep on doing it, the AA way."

"But there's nothing I can do tonight."

"You tell me that you're taking your inventory."

So I told her that I was grateful to her. I told her that she had been wonderful to come. We had a quiet talk and she left.

That night before falling asleep I saw that the faults I had objected to in Dick were, substantially, the faults I had myself. In the next few days I worked on myself, not on Dick. Spiritual insight is wonderful—painful at times, but wonderful. And I could see, with a further reach of insight, that Dick and I were indeed meant for one another. A power greater than ourselves had brought us together, and I had been returned to Philadelphia, because in this way I could work out problems that I had run away from, and learn a mature way of life that I had always avoided.

I saw how closely we were bound in heart and mind. We had the same interests, the same background, with similar assets and liabilities. We loved one another. Dick had never really lost sight of this. He had tried to help me. When he himself seemed unlovable, wasn't that when he needed love the most?

The next day Dick told me that he had been taking his own inventory. He was kind, for he didn't say: "Unassisted by you."

We decided that our shared life was pretty wonderful. Since then the dividends have been pouring in. Have we lived happily ever after, with never a cross word? Of course not, we are only human and, being alcoholics, we are, as they say, slightly more so. But our rows aren't as hair-raising, our cross-fire inventories aren't as hostile. Dick has taught me that gentle, well-timed praise is worth a pound of blame.

I can laugh at myself. Dick has a radiant sense of humor, a fine mind. We help each other with our work, when help is needed, when encouragement is needed. And we have an increasing circle of friends, old and new, plus a lively interest in our new neighbors. The other night we joined a citizen's committee to help our rapidly improving neighborhood. Best of all, I still don't agree with some of Dick's actions and opinions, but I am relieved of the burden of having to live his life for him. The God of Dick's understanding is right there with him, guiding him and showing him the way.

We talk quite often of starting a double Al-Anon, to be known as A-Square. Any customers?

(Ed. note—Initials, names and locales in the foregoing have been changed for added anonymity-protection.)

K. W.
Philadelphia, Pennsylvania

CHAPTER THREE

Dating and Romance

Getting out there and navigating the dating game without a glass in hand

" began every relationship in a web of lies," writes Jeff H. in the story "Relationships Reconsidered," as he describes what happens when dating meets drinking. In "With or Without Him," Jan A. says drinking led her to fall in love with one guy for his snakeskin boots, and with another because he had sad eyes.

But early sobriety can be an equally volatile playing field, as we see in this section on dating and romance. "Two garbage trucks colliding" is many a tough sponsor's description of newcomers romancing each other. "With a hostile divorce looming, a rented room I called home, a rusty pickup for wheels ... few clothes ... erratic work ... and six months of sobriety in AA, I didn't get why beautiful women wouldn't consider me a real find," admits one writer in "Hey There, Lonely Guy." He was "a 14-year-old in a 35-year-old body" in his early days, says another member, while he airily—and hilariously—dismisses good advice, calling it a product of his sponsor's "threadbare libido."

"I was 14 when I went looking for love. I found a bottle instead," says K.T. in "Looking for Love," who adds that years of coupling never taught her how to be half of a couple. Twelve Steps later, she knows how.

Relationships Reconsidered

Grapevine Online Exclusive – November 2013

When I got sober in 1999, I had been married for just 18 months and arrived in the rooms on what you might call a "wife card." I hadn't gone to jail, wasn't homeless, and was still successful in my employment.

Everything from the outside was "looking good!" So, naturally, I figured I was not as bad off as all of you and therefore didn't need to do everything that was suggested. It made sense to me ... as a good, stubborn and sick alcoholic in full denial, I refused to work the Steps or keep a sponsor, nevermind "practice these principles" in any of my affairs.

Although I stayed sober, my life continued to spiral out of control until I was faced with being fired from my wonderful job. Only at this point, did I surrender completely to the program of Alcoholics Anonymous in its entirety.

As a result, I thoroughly completed my Steps with a sponsor. I came to realize that I began every relationship with a web of lies. My second wife had once called me a chameleon ... and I was so offended! Only in the examination of my behavior in doing the Steps did I see how true her words were.

I would become attracted to a woman and begin the deception. I would act and behave in ways that I thought she wanted me to. If she were going to church, I'd go to church. My attire would change and my tastes would change. All to be the man I thought she wanted. I had always felt insecure and unworthy, subconsciously believing that the right woman would make that better. I knew if these women found out the truth about me, they'd run screaming.

Although my life began to change for the better in sobriety, my marriage still ended and I was forced to file for bankruptcy and endure long-term unemployment. In the midst of this seemingly tragic chain of events, I was asked by a friend to take his place in helping to open our meeting because he didn't want the woman who was the meeting leader to be there at 5 A.M. alone.

I agreed without really knowing the woman, other than the fact that she was quite attractive. As the months passed, we became close and started seeing each other socially. I remembered hearing some old-timers talking about people in recovery dating other people in recovery. They remarked how insane it was for two insane people to date one another. I was nine years sober at the time and she had two years, but we quickly became trudging buddies. As our relationship began to grow I continued reflecting on my history and focusing on the man I wanted to become.

In this process, I paid close attention to my sex inventory. I looked at how I had aroused suspicion and jealousy by being too friendly with other women, how I was dishonest and self-seeking, and how I focused my attention on ensuring my needs were met.

I also reflected on how I would divert attention away from whatever I was doing wrong in the relationship by pointing my finger at the woman in my life. I started paying some attention to the definition of love as described by my religion. Love was supposed to be patient, kind, not jealous, and unselfish. These concepts and the vast change that would be required in me seemed insurmountable, but the woman I had met so quickly after ending a marriage seemed like such a perfect match that I couldn't imagine finding another.

My first opportunity to do something different came very soon. I had been shopping at our local mall alone and called to invite her to join me. When she arrived my head started in. I thought, What if I run into some friends from my previous marriage? What will people think? (The insanity of my thinking doesn't stop with time!) The result was complete discomfort, which was very visible and obvious to her.

Needless to say, it was an unpleasant venture, leaving her feeling awful. What did I do differently? I spoke to this woman about how I felt and what was running through my mind. I made direct amends to her quickly and have not repeated that behavior since. I practiced what AA had taught me.

My second huge obstacle was being completely honest with her. I struggled with the fear of losing her and had to ask myself some very important questions. Does she have a right to know the complete truth about me? Does she deserve to make her own decision to stay or leave this relationship based on the facts? Although I decided that I loved her too much not to tell her the truth, it didn't make it easy. Despite my thinking, she did not run for the hills. In fact, she knew there was something I wanted to divulge. Again, I practiced the tenets of this wonderful program.

I have also changed the ways I interacted with other women, both in and out of the rooms. I do not ignore them, but I maintain a very respectful distance. I never want to arouse that suspicion and jealousy which was previously a part of my life. I no longer need the attention of other women to make me feel worthwhile at the expense of the woman I love.

This relationship has proven to be the best ever. Our success relies on our own personal recovery path and practicing the principles of AA in our relationship. When she is doing something that annoys me, I immediately ask myself, What is going on with me that I find it so difficult to accept her for who she is? By continuing to trust God and clean house, this relationship is completely effortless. We do not try to work each other's program and we respect each other's anonymity, along with that of the people we sponsor.

I have learned much since embarking on this journey, and there's still a lot more to learn so I remain teachable. Therefore, I listen to my girlfriend today, without feeling like I need to "fix" her. I also tell her how I feel about things and work through the fears of being vulnerable. This is a continuous process for me and I hope never to think I have arrived. Today I trust, I love, and I have faith in a power greater than me. Today I am free from the bondage of self and hopefully have become more loving in the process.

Jeff H.
Lancaster, California

Happily Together In Recovery

February 2003

By the time I arrived in AA, I had been burnt in all of my relationships (although I admit I lit the flame myself a few times), and I wasn't interested in ever dating again. At four years sober, I did start dating again, both in and out of the program, but I still wasn't very interested. One friend from my home group, 20 years my senior and recently divorced, used to join me for breakfast once or twice a week before our meeting, and we'd share our funny dating tales. Did we laugh! You know, after several months of this, we realized that our friendship could develop into something else. We began dating each other, and tried to take it slowly.

We're still together, very happily, nearly nine years later. We learned a lot of lessons along the way. We learned that we couldn't belong to the same home group, and that only occasionally could we go to meetings together. We each needed to maintain our own program, and when we were in an AA meeting, our focus needed to be on the meeting itself. When we were a new couple, we were too focused on each other to get anything out of a meeting. We learned that in the relationship, our friendship was the most valuable thing we had, and that our romantic inclinations were secondary to the friendship. We learned not to call one another's sponsor. We learned not to try to sponsor one another. We learned to pray together. We learned to be honest with one another. We learned to cherish one another. In AA, we find lives we never could have imagined. I also found the kind of relationship I didn't know I could have.

I think that if two people in the Fellowship keep their recovery primary and central in their lives, and have some solid recovery time behind them, they *can* date each other without disaster unfolding. While it is true that we are in AA because we have a disease that can wreak complete havoc in our lives, it is also true that we are working on a solution. As long as the solution, rather than our relationship, is central in our lives, we can achieve true partnership.

Anonymous

Looking for Love
March 1984

was 14 when I first went looking for love. I found a bottle instead. I wanted so much to be needed and cared for. I wanted someone to feel they had the whole world in their arms when they held me. I wanted to belong to someone. From the time I was 14, I needed alcohol to give me the courage to trade my body for love. I was living in such a dreamworld that I never knew it wasn't love I was getting until it was almost too late.

When I was 30, I had three marriages behind me, and I was living with a 21-year-old man. One night, the same old tape was playing that had played so many times before: I was drunk, feeling unloved, afraid he was going to leave, and I said some terrible things to him. I loved him, and yet I had to hurt him before he hurt me. What happened to me that night was a miracle. For the first time in my life, I thought maybe the reason my insatiable need for love was not being met was something wrong in me.

That was the beginning. I went to AA. But it was not a cure. When I was three months sober, I was two months pregnant—a direct result of thirteenth-stepping. I didn't have alcohol in me now, but I was still looking for love in the wrong way. By the grace of God, I didn't have to live with that mistake, but I didn't learn from it, either.

For nearly five years, I continued to compromise my self-respect in return for a little attention. My life was one continuous heartbreak, and I never realized, as I had five years before, that it might be my fault. I centered all my efforts on men in AA. Then I rationalized that that was my problem, and I married a man outside AA. That marriage lasted six months. I just couldn't make anything click. I had done and tried everything. I gave up!

And that's when it happened. That's when my whole life became a dream come true. It didn't happen overnight, however. It took application of the Twelve Steps specifically to the area of my life that had been giving me so much trouble. It took a lot of prayer and meditation, and a year of celibacy.

In that year, I read everything I could and listened to everyone I could, to find my own understanding of God. I became as obsessive about that as I had been about looking for love. It's ironic, isn't it—how you can be looking for the same thing on two totally different paths? I discovered that God is love. God helped me to see that I was love, and that if I was love, I didn't have to search for it anymore. And lo and behold, when I quit searching, there he was! This man was absolutely nothing like the lover I had pictured, but then God knows better than I, without exception. There was no trade. We didn't need one. We both had what we wanted, and when we came together, it was a union that I never dreamed could exist.

We're celebrating our first wedding anniversary soon, and for me, it is literally my first. In all my earlier marriages, I never made it to a first anniversary. Without the patience and understanding of my friends in AA, I never could have made it this time either. I couldn't have stayed sober without the acceptance that I found in AA. I'd like to add a special thanks to Ala-Fam; that's like an AA meeting for couples. In all my years of coupling, I never learned how to be half of a couple!

If you are just finding sobriety, and feel life lacks the love that should be there, let me share this with you: Don't look for love—discover it!

K. T.

Naples, Florida

Hey There, Lonely Guy
February 2008

My pattern was always the same. I'd ambush my intended quarry and ask for a date. Hot on the scent, I'd sprint through the preliminaries—a movie, dinner, a walk in the woods, a late-night phone call or two—then charge into the sack for some urgent relating. Three or four weeks of eternal love later, we'd argue about something I don't remember. Not too long after that, she'd start acting like I was in the way.

With a hostile divorce looming, a rented room I called home, a rusty pickup for wheels, a few changes of work clothes for a wardrobe, erratic self-employment, and six months of sobriety in AA, I didn't get why beautiful women wouldn't consider me a real find, an awesome candidate for their longtime partner, and a father for their children.

When I complained about yet another failed romance, my sponsor would repeat, wearily, "The way you get through a divorce is: One day at a time, you keep it simple, clean up the wreckage of your past, and stay out of relationships." Crucial as his guidance was on everything alcoholic, at 62, he was obviously way too old to understand the needs of a young, imaginative, energetic guy like me, or why I was different from all those middle-aged trolls in AA grousing about no relationships for a year. I mean, a year? Why not just join a monastery?

Okay, I was clueless. I had no idea what a relationship with a woman or, for that matter, with anyone, should look like. Growing up around my house, where Dad drank every day until he died from a drunken auto accident, I learned that a man was supposed to know everything, work real hard, and provide all the financial resources. This gave us the right to drink—as long as we stayed in control—and to make all major decisions, regardless of what anybody else thought or felt—and who cares how anybody feels, anyway?

Men sober longer than I confessed they'd never been in a relationship; they'd only taken hostages. I couldn't identify. Being a smart, creative, sensitive guy with great potential, now that I wasn't drinking, I just wanted my prospective partner to know how fortunate she was to hook somebody who could show her how to do everything the right way.

I'd read that stuff in the "Twelve and Twelve" about being too dependent on others or expecting them to be dependent on me, and the metaphor in the Big Book about being an actor who was happy only when directing the whole show. But I couldn't relate to that. I just wanted others to recognize the good intentions motivating my gratuitous advice, and to get over whatever their problem was with my being direct and authoritative. After all, getting things done required a man to be decisive and firm.

So my pattern was always the same. Bulldoze my way through a date or two, pole vault into the big bed, fall deeply, enduringly in love for three weeks, outlast an argument or two (or three), hear dwindling interest on the other end of the phone when I called, wonder what could be so wrong with this woman that she didn't see the gift God brought her, and slip out the back before getting my walking papers. There was always something better down the road, anyway.

Three years, three Fourth and Fifth Steps, and about 10 months of white-knuckle celibacy later (just to prove it wouldn't work), I was approached by a bright, beautiful woman I'd been tracking at meetings for a few weeks. She told me how comforting it was to see me coming regularly for the year-and-a-half she'd been attending (I'd noticed her only a few weeks before) and that I looked like I needed a hug.

I had never once thought of myself as "needing a hug." Friendship, like my family relationships, was never a contact sport. Also, I was in the middle of a three-month, intensive, out-patient program for adult children of alcoholics; my sponsor had died several months before; and, thanks to AA and two good therapists, I was painfully aware of my lack of social skills and my underlying fear that triggered my sometimes gracious, sometimes blatant manipulation for control.

So, "No thanks," didn't register on the radar. Or, "How about a handshake for today, and it's real nice to see you, too." Forget about it. I answered with a big, brilliant, "Whatever." She gave me a quick squeeze and pulled back looking perplexed, as if she'd expected more, but smiled. And the whole front of my body melted and congealed like bad wiring after a surge has burnt away the insulation. I may have smiled, but I clearly remember feeling dumber than I ever have before or since, as if my self-will had blown a fuse and I had no alternate source of power.

And that's the story of when, at 38 years old and three years sober, I learned what lonely feels like, and how it's different from horny. Lonely murmurs: Patience; time; acceptance; let go; thy will, not mine. Horny cries out like a starving seagull: MORE! MORE! MORE! The wrestling match was on: Thy will or my will?

Here was one small lesson learned and one small step forward for one muddled soul stumbling in the darkness. That bright, beautiful woman and I have been together the better part of 20 years now, married for 12 of them.

Anyone who's listened to AA stories as if his life depended on it knows there's no happily ever after in sobriety. These past 20 years have certainly been proof enough—but that's not the point. It's hearing, at long last, the quiet inner voice that murmurs: Patience; time; acceptance; let go; thy will, not mine. That's the point.

And without Alcoholics Anonymous inside my life—inside our life together—I'd still be the callow, clueless, overly gracious, passive-aggressive control freak who, to this day, sometimes still wants to be right. Me, I'd rather be married. But that's just for today.

Anonymous

With or Without Him

February 2008

Before I started to drink, through childhood, and throughout my drinking career, I was desperately—pathetically—lonely. I hated being in my skin. I believe drinking saved my life when I was younger, because I couldn't live with myself without the drink. When it turned on me later, I could barely live with myself at all.

When I quit drinking, I still didn't know how to live with myself. I didn't have to—I jumped right into a relationship. At the time, I thought I was working the Steps, but I didn't have a sponsor and was barely going to one meeting a week. By the time he and I broke up, I was not going to meetings at all. Alone again, I wanted to drink, badly. I was just over a year sober and I was miserable. I thought I would never have love in my life, would never have children, and would never fit in. To be single at my advanced age meant I had failed as a woman and a person. I was 29.

I got up the nerve and finally went back to meetings, three or four a week. Slowly, I made friends and became part of the Fellowship. I got a sponsor and started doing service. Later, I attended AA dances, hung out at the clubhouse, and did other social things. A nagging loneliness persisted when I came home to my empty apartment. I adopted a cat.

At around 18 months sober, I met F. He convinced me we should start going out, even though he had fewer than 10 months sober. He said—correctly—that there was no "AA rule" that said we couldn't date.

I went out with F. against my sponsor's advice, and she fired me. I thought it was worth it; I thought I was in love. I had never learned how to have a relationship. F. filled my needs. And damn, I was needy. After several months, the more I needed to be together, the more he needed to be alone. The further away he got from his last drink, the better he felt, and the less he needed me. Six months after the relationship started, he dumped me. Ouch.

I spent the next six months or so crying and moaning about my pain in meetings and with anyone who would listen. (I try to remember how annoying I was when others share about relationships today.) It seemed everyone else was married with children. I believed that I wasn't "normal"; that I was "unlovable"; that God had punished me.

Around that time, M. became my new sponsor. She told me that there was a solution to my misery, and that we were going to do the Steps using the Big Book. I had done some Step work by then, but with M., I started over. Just about everyone I knew was on my resentment list. The reasons were ridiculous: "she has a baby"; "she's getting married"; "he rejected me." What did this affect? My self-esteem, my personal relationships, my pride (fear). What was I afraid of? Being alone. Being different. Aha.

In my sex inventory I saw that I had been selfish in every one of my relationships. My sponsor said, however, that I was going to be OK, because I was going to ask God to mold my ideals and help me work toward them.

"Get out of yourself and go help someone else," she said. When I wanted to wallow in my grief, she dragged me to AA dances, where we'd see F. with his new girlfriend. I hated that. "Think about what you can bring to a situation, not what you can get out of it," she said. She'd point out a man sitting by himself and she'd make me go ask him to dance. At meetings, she told me to introduce myself to new women and take them for coffee afterward. When I did (I was often stubborn), it worked, and I felt less miserable.

I made lots of mistakes. Eventually, I dated one guy because I liked his snakeskin boots; another because he played guitar and had sad eyes; another because he rode a motorcycle.

In my Ninth Step work, M. told me that part of my amends meant changing what I'd always done in relationships. I had a hard time being OK with myself, alone. I would debate with M.: "What if it's God's will that I have to be alone for the rest of my life?"

She would say, "It's God's will that you don't drink, and I also believe he wants us to be happy. It's natural for people to want relationships. Work on the Steps and work toward finding a healthy relationship." She never said I shouldn't date, she just said to pray for the guidance to do the right thing.

I filled up my life with AA service work. I also joined a bowling league made up of AAs, I adopted a second cat, and I dated here and there. But I never formed a long-term relationship with anyone. I wondered if it was God's will, and if I was ready to accept it.

During this time, my sponsor moved to another state.

I then entered into a relationship, at about five years sober, that nearly destroyed my sanity and my sobriety. J., who had 15 years without a drink, took possession of me immediately. I got swept up in the romance.

No one had treated me this nicely in a long time. No one had made me feel this pretty, this smart, this special. He was so romantic.

And then he became controlling, as well as emotionally and physically abusive. There were apologies, forgiveness, more romance, and then more control and abuse. I forgave J., because "this was love." Soon, he was running my life—with my permission. Because of his demands, I started skipping service commitments. "If you are in a relationship, your focus should be on that relationship. You can't be out every night," he said.

I quit the bowling league and gradually dropped every service position I held. I dropped friends because I was embarrassed about J.'s hold on me. After several unsuccessful attempts to leave him, I moved across the country—but ended up back with him 10 months later. Then, he convinced me to move away from my New Jersey family and friends, and we ended up in Florida. Although we were both going to AA meetings the whole time, I can't say I was working much of a program.

An AA friend told me that I was using J. as my God. She said, "You're saying that you don't trust God to take care of you. God does not want you to be this miserable." But God must have been taking care of me, because I still didn't drink in spite of the insanity.

One morning, after a bad night, I simply decided I'd had enough. I believe it was another spiritual awakening. It was the beginning of a new recovery. When I first came to AA, I thought the craving for alcohol would never go away. Leaving J. felt the same way. In spite of the pain, I had been terrified to leave, thinking I would never be OK without a man in my life; I would never be OK with just "me." I asked God for help and prayed for strength to be on my own.

I was single for about five years after that. I felt scarred, but gradually got better. I got a new sponsor, and she helped me in several areas: One, that in my recovery, I didn't have to be perfect; two, that being single didn't mean I had failed; and three, that other people would accept me the way I was.

The summer I turned 40, I moved to New York City. It was a great place to be single. There were so many different types and combinations of people that I didn't feel weird not being married with children. I had often felt that way in the suburbs of my native southern New Jersey, where I'd gotten sober.

I wasn't a saint, though—I still thought it would be nice to have a steady man in my life! A mutual friend said P. and I should hook up. We went for sushi and immediately I liked him. He was a kind person—but also funny, intelligent, attractive, and oddly "normal." I didn't know if I deserved him, but I wanted to be with him. The crazy thing was that he felt the same way about me.

So, it just happened. I wasn't looking for a relationship, but I wasn't not looking, either. I wasn't spiritually sound, but I wasn't all that spiritually unsound, either. Some days I still hated being in my own skin—but mostly I loved myself. All I did was not drink, go to meetings, and help others when I could. The program of AA brought me to where I was comfortable with myself. Our wedding day was one of the happiest days of my life.

I love P., he makes me happy, and he tolerates my two cats sharing our crammed apartment. I recently committed myself to four meetings a week and two service positions. P. is not in AA, and at first I was afraid that he wouldn't like me going out that much, but he understands that this is important to me. He accepts me!

Life is good. But, since I don't know what God's plan is, I may be single, again, at some point. But today, I have a lot of hope that I won't be drinking over it.

Jan A.

Queens, New York

Prime Dating Material?

February 2008

When I got sober, one of the first things I heard in AA was that I had stopped maturing when I started drinking. If this was true, I was a 15-year-old in a 37-year-old body, and it meant that, along with the other difficulties of new sobriety, I had to experience being a teenager again—but this time without alcohol.

I started drinking in order to set myself at ease socially, first at high school dances, then at parties, then at bars and nightclubs, and finally at home, alone. I probably never had a relationship with a girl that didn't start and end with booze and drugs. Sober sex was not on my agenda.

I spent the next 22 years as a wannabe musician, paying my bills by way of illegal business ventures. I never dated—I either had toxic relationships or cruised the night spots like a predator, looking for the combination of the perfect high and that stunning, successful, articulate woman who was going to change my world. My standards inevitably got lower as the evening got closer to last call.

So, when I finally got to Alcoholics Anonymous, completely wrecked, broke, scared, in trouble with the law, unemployable, and alone, I didn't have much faith in a shining future. The party was over, and I didn't have a clue how to live a regular life. I wound up living at my parents' house. I got a crummy job, a nice little $200 newcomer's car, and I went to meetings. My teeth were bad and soon my clothes didn't fit—I carried 30 pounds of AA cookies and doughnuts around my waist. Boy, was I ever prime dating material!

At one year sober, I got involved in what I now (affectionately) call Big Book boot camp in a church in Ocean Park, California. We were on fire, sharing about doing the work, writing massive inventories, and learning to carry the message. Meanwhile, I had dabbled a bit in sober dating. I was shy, awkward, and not very interested in anyone who would have me.

Then it happened—I found her! I was delirious, totally in over my head, and ready to move in with her at the drop of a hat. After two dates and two weeks, she told me that she was back with her boyfriend. I was crushed. Didn't she know what she was missing? How could she have led me on this way? What did he have that I didn't have (besides a real job and a high-end sports car)?

Fortunately, people in AA consoled me and consistently redirected my attention to my primary purpose. They told me that romance would happen in God's time, not necessarily in my time. They told me that I couldn't expect to be made whole by another person—that the Steps and a spiritual awakening would solve my problems. I listened to them and surrendered my desire to be in a relationship. I launched into Steps with renewed vigor and felt a new freedom, as I was no longer on the prowl when I went to meetings.

A few months went by. One night, I was at a local speaker meeting, minding my own business, enjoying the group with no other expectation than to be present for an evening of sobriety. When the meeting ended, I joined the line to thank the speaker, as I had been taught. A woman I hadn't seen before was in line in front of me. She was tall, attractive, and well-dressed. After she thanked the speaker, she hung around and we wound up introducing ourselves. I didn't plan this, but after exchanging names, I found myself asking, "Do you work the Steps?" Now there's a lame pick-up line if I ever heard one, but she cheerfully answered, "Yes."

We went for coffee soon after, then met at some other local meetings, and finally went on a date. I spent way more than I could afford, but we laughed and joked and had such a good time together that it was worth it.

Over the next few weeks, I had to compete with a few others who were interested in her (she was new in town). Once again, I experienced discomfort, but what she did was none of my business, so I kept my mouth shut. Meanwhile, I brought her to my Big Book meeting in Ocean Park and she committed to re-taking the Steps at three years sober.

Thank God my sponsor in that group cared enough about me to make sure I didn't skip the sex inventory! After answering the questions in the middle of page 69 (where had I been selfish and dishonest?, where was I at fault?, etc.), I asked myself, What should I have done instead? The answers were the opposite of what I had typically done: Where I had been dishonest, tell the truth; where I had been selfish, be giving; where I had been inconsiderate, be thoughtful. From this, I was able to mold an ideal, as the book says. It was helpful to write it out in a couple of paragraphs—this provided me with a template for future conduct that I could always refer to (and ask for the power to live up to.)

I am grateful that the opportunity to contribute on this theme came up in Grapevine. Whenever I speak in front of large groups, telling my AA story, I have been forced to stop each time I reach the part about meeting the woman in the line to thank the speaker. I become overwhelmed with gratitude. I have to wave my hands around and hold back tears until I am able to use my voice again. It's 19 years later; we are married and have two beautiful children who have never seen us drink or use abusive language toward each other.

I have been miraculously relieved of my old behaviors and attitudes regarding relationships with women, and have been truly blessed to have experienced the closeness, finally, that I had always searched for.

Dan H.
Oceanside, California

———————————————

Me and You and AA
Grapevine Online Exclusive – November 2013

At a point during my recovery, my boyfriend, Paul, who is also sober, decided we needed to take some space from each other and live apart. I was working full-time and going to school full-time. Paul had an adult son struggling with addiction and another son testing the waters. We both had financial stress. He and I began to focus more and more on outside influences and less on our own recovery. We became unhealthy for ourselves and for each other.

Prior to our breakup, I still managed to make one or two meetings a week, but it wasn't enough. I stopped attending therapy and exercising. I failed to reach out to my sponsor and my girlfriends. I made Paul my entire support system. In his words, "he was supporting me and yet he couldn't support himself." It was a pretty accurate portrayal of our dynamic.

While I respected his decision, it was a heartbreaking, horrible, devastating time. I was in love with this man and thought we were spending the rest of our lives together. I sat on the couch and cried for three hours. After begging, groveling, making empty promises and watching my dignity and self-respect fly out the window, I picked up that one-ton phone and called a girlfriend in recovery.

She picked me up, bought me a calorie-laden cup of hot caffeine deliciousness and took me to a womens' meeting. I cried the whole time ... but I managed to fall asleep sober that night. The next day I took a shower, hit a noon meeting and went to work.

After work I went to another meeting. That second night I cried myself to sleep after three meetings ... but again, I fell asleep sober. In that first week, I went to at least a meeting every day, sometimes many more than that. I cried every time I felt like crying. I desperately wanted just a moment of relief from the pain and obsessive thoughts of worry, remorse and morbid reflection but instead I felt it all, one minute at a time. I showed up on campus and took my finals for the semester. I didn't do as well as I hoped to but I managed to get a "C" or better in all four of my classes.

Every time I wanted to call or text Paul, I called a woman in the program instead. I blew up my phone getting to know the amazing women I had spent so long ignoring or pushing away. The women in AA are a gift from God and I never could have made it through gracefully without them.

One took me to yoga within 48 hours of the breakup. We went ice-skating and discovered amazing sushi restaurants. They gave me makeovers and highlighted my hair. We drank endless cups of coffee and they listened without judgment. One let me sleep on her air mattress for over a month until I found my own place. On New Year's Eve seven of them kidnapped me and took me to a meeting out-of-town. At midnight I went outside the meeting, hit my knees and prayed to a God I was angry with.

As an alcoholic, I'm very good at walking toward the pain. This one time I decided to walk away from it. I found different coffee shops and different meetings. I was given the gift of a massage on my birthday.

I went sky-diving for the first time on Christmas and then ate a huge breakfast with my sky-diving buddy. I had no idea what my ex was doing at this point because I respected myself and him enough to give him the space he asked for. I couldn't see him in person without crying so I set healthy boundaries. We communicated via email when communication was necessary and we kept our emails friendly.

When I moved out I asked him not to be at home and he respected me by being elsewhere. We both owned our part and never—OK, almost never—said an unkind word about the other. We made it clear to our many, many mutual friends that we would not listen to criticism of the other person or the taking of sides. We kept our sides of the street clean.

Today, Paul and I are friends because of the actions we both took in those first difficult weeks. We might start dating again, while living apart, but that remains to be seen. I go to a womens' meeting every Saturday morning. My therapist and I are back together on a weekly basis. I'm still in college working on my degree in anthropology. Between classes I call my girlfriends or my sponsee or my sponsor from the treadmill at the campus recreation center. I'm still with that same employer who was so patient with me. Friday mornings I get together with my best friend in the program for prayer and daily readings. I make at least four meetings every week. Paul takes care of himself in ways that are different than mine but no less important.

Crucially, neither one of us drank over it and for two people in recovery, that's a gift of our spirituality and the Fellowship of AA.

Liz P.

Tempe, Arizona

Letting Go of the Golden Glow

Grapevine Online Exclusive – April 2014

Last Christmas Eve was the 40th anniversary of my coming out as the gay man I always was but could never allow myself to be because of shame and guilt over what I thought was the most perverse of perversions. My coming out was a gift of sobriety and occurred a little more than two years after I made a decision, at my first meeting, to try this thing called one-day-at-a-time sobriety. That end to daily drinking, which I have maintained ever since through the grace of God, was my first gift from God and Alcoholics Anonymous.

I was raised to believe that men loved women and you had to hit them once in a while or they wouldn't respect you. I came of age in the 1950s when there was no support for being gay. There were no openly gay celebrities and politicians and no gay pride parades. Gay people, or those thought to be, were teased, beaten, arrested or killed.

I wanted nothing more than to become heterosexual and whenever I had a good relationship with a woman, I thought it was happening. But whenever I was with a woman, I was thinking about—and looking at—men. My few contacts with men, usually when drunk, filled me with fear and self-loathing.

After being sober for a while, I realized that a lot of my drinking was over the tension, anger, frustration and resentment engendered by living a lie about something as powerful as sex. I was forced to pretend and deny. When out with the guys, I joined in the jokes and the belittling of gays to make sure they knew I was as macho as they were. Inside, I felt like a shameful coward.

As with so many alcoholics, drinking seemed to be the answer to my problems when I started at 18 in college. With the right number of drinks, I was bathed in a golden glow that made everything wonderful. Fear, depression, anxiety, social awkwardness and any thoughts that I was an unworthy pervert vanished. But, of course, that was a temporary state, and when it wore off I was left with terrible hangovers and everything I'd been escaping from with alcohol came back.

When I read Chapter Three in the Big Book, I found myself—the drinker determined to control and enjoy his drinking. I wanted to achieve that golden glow without getting too drunk so I could go about my business, never realizing that it was impossible because of the nature of alcoholism. Once an alcoholic takes a drink, the drink decides what happens next and it usually says keep on drinking. Control is an illusion.

For the most part, I was a solitary drinker at home. When I began getting in trouble in public during the last six months of my drinking—embarrassing people, getting tossed out of places, risking assault or arrest, endangering my job—I reached my incomprehensible and demoralizing state of alcoholism. I knew there was a better way to live but I didn't know how to find it.

Then, through a series of events that I called coincidences but now know was God doing for me what I couldn't do for myself, I was taken to an AA meeting by a friend. By the time that first meeting ended, I knew that AA was where I needed to be. God gave me the gift of sobriety and I became willing to work to keep it.

I was sober but I was still determined to become straight or dismiss sex altogether. Fat chance, because it's too strong a human drive. But as I grew in sobriety, and found a Higher Power of my understanding, my attitudes about myself began to change. My first sponsor was everything I wasn't—Republican, conservative, businessman, straight, husband and father. When I unloaded my sexual conflicts in all their sordid detail, I waited for him to order me out of his house—or to kick me down the stairs because he lived on the second floor. But he loved me all the more. That's when I knew that "we care" is true and that anyone desiring sobriety, no matter who or what he is, is welcome in AA.

He was the first person I had ever spoken to about these issues with honesty and openness. He told me that however God made me was OK. God loves all of us just the way we come down the chute. But I wasn't ready yet.

In the months before my Christmas Eve emergence, I became close to a gay man who was very happy being who he was after struggling to overcome his religious upbringing. We had long talks, during which I became increasingly willing to be with my own kind, to stop lying and denying.

I had to stop thinking about what I was taught and what society accepts or condemns and look at who I was, a man who happens to love men. Gay liberation was underway by then, gay people were increasingly open, and I had to liberate myself. I remembered what that sponsor told me about God loving everyone just the way they were created. I knew that homosexuality was innate, not a choice, so it wasn't unnatural, immoral or wrong. It just was.

I call Christmas Eve, 1972, my coming out because it was the first time I was with a man because I really wanted to be with a man. I felt no shame, guilt, remorse or self-condemnation. The man I was with was a gentle soul, the perfect guide into my new and honest identity, and he made me feel wonderful.

Has being sober and gay always been a state of bliss? No. I've had to deal with problems of trust, intimacy and letting another human being completely into my life. I've had a weakness for needy people who have nothing to offer in return. I've learned painfully that some men only want to see you once. I've given my heart to people who didn't want it. I've been possessive and manipulative in vain attempts to hold onto people. I've experienced the anxiety that comes with obsessing over someone you think you can't live without and fear losing. But I've never taken a drink over any of it and, obviously, I haven't killed myself. And I don't think any of this is about being gay. It's about being human.

Jerry F.

Cerritos, California

Saturday Night

May 2008

A while back, I was sitting at a neighborhood AA meeting on a Saturday evening when a woman I knew took a seat across from me. I was dressed in plain clothes, whereas she had on an evening dress. A feeling of embarrassment and vulnerability came over me. I waved to her self-consciously. Suddenly, I feared she was seeing something I hadn't wanted her to see, that I was alone and had no place else to go. She left at the break. I imagined that it was her way of saying she had plans for the evening. Of course I did have someplace else to go. I went to a store, where I purchased some groceries, and headed home.

Is Saturday night the loneliest night of the week, as the song says? Sometimes, yes. And yet our Big Book says we have to be willing to let go of old ideas, and the old idea that sometimes revisits me is that I am supposed to be with someone on a Saturday night. However, the reality is that, more and more, I am not. I am with myself. Of course, I am no longer in my thirties or even forties, when the matter of relationships can take on a real intensity.

My first home group met on a Saturday night. I would arrive early for the hospitality setup and experience intense joy in going about the simple task of making coffee and laying out the cookies in an arrangement I fussily protected. Having performed my service, I would then sit contentedly through the beginners' meeting and the open discussion meeting that followed.

Though a quarter century has passed, I remember very clearly a man from that group. He spoke in balanced sentences, with not a word out of place. Alcohol had robbed him of his executive-level position, but not his manifest intelligence. A detail from his story that remains with me was that in his last year of drinking, he often wore dirty clothes to the office and used screws and bolts on his shirts as a substitute for the cufflinks he had lost.

But the more pertinent memory I have is of him following an attractive woman out of the meeting place after the closing prayer. His frantic pursuit signaled his interest in her. A few minutes later, he was back. Evidently, his attempt at connection had been unsuccessful, and now there was a look of desperation in his eyes as he sought out some other woman in the group whose company would spare him the loneliness of another sober Saturday night by himself.

The man had gone on with his drinking longer than I had. There had been time for alcoholism to take more from him than it had from me. I was 10 or 15 years younger than the man and had a wife to go home to that night. His loneliness stayed in my mind. He was telling me something about the difficulty of being single or divorced and getting sober in middle age. I felt relieved to know that I would never be in his social situation.

My wife and I separated when I was sober two-and-a-half years. Within six months, I was living with another woman, and a year later, we married. This second marriage continued into my 10th year of recovery. With newfound marital stability, I developed an unspoken attitude of superiority in the matter of relationships. There seemed to be so many men and women in the Fellowship who couldn't find a partner or, if they did, the matches were fleeting things that fell apart within a week or a month. Such poor, stymied, unfortunate souls, so damaged that they couldn't establish a meaningful connection with another human being. Well, better them than me, I thought.

My second marriage had represented a sort of finish line that I had crossed into endless emotional as well as financial security, and when the rupture occurred, the experience was extremely painful. On some level, I was a newcomer all over again, a man aged 42 living alone for the first time in close to 20 years.

I began traveling on my own, two- and three-week journeys to different parts of Europe. In these travels, as at home, I would see couples and actually disparage them in my mind. Look at these poor, crippled souls, I would think. They can't spend two hours out of each others' sight. How clinging. How sad. Thoughts of this kind were to visit me many times in the succeeding years. If I saw a man and his wife in the AA rooms, I would think the same thing. From a place of smug superiority in my married life vis-a-vis single people, I had now, as a man living alone, adopted this same disparaging attitude toward men and women in relationships. In both cases, it was simply a matter of my ego reserving the right to feel superior to the rest of humankind. Evidently, a program of ego deflation is not a program that leads to the ego's disappearance.

This lofty dismissal of the human urge to connect notwithstanding, I would invariably meet some woman in my travels, and on the basis of only the slightest contact, find myself ravaged by an obsession that was seldom reciprocated, in which every cell of my being would scream in longing for this new object of my desire.

In the second year of my marital separation, I finally took off my wedding band and placed it under the base of the lamp on the dresser in my bedroom. Now, driven by dreams of sex more than romance, I was free to seek out the company of women in the Fellowship and beyond the rooms. From one meeting to the next I would trek, choosing those where I thought my chances of hooking up with Ms. Right were optimal, just as, in my drinking days, I had gone from bar to bar in the drunken hope of sexual adventure. More often than not, AA women would say no when I asked them out, but now and then one would agree.

Then, one evening, I ran into a woman who was new to my home group on the street outside the meeting place. The next night we met for dinner. She was warm and funny as well as beautiful, but she was, as it turned out, only six months sober. And though I made every effort to stay away for this reason, she dominated my every thought and within four months we were seeing each other.

The relationship with this AA woman lasted for about 15 months. I was 46 and 14 years sober, while she was at least 12 years younger. I was to learn that the AA saying, "Don't get involved with a newcomer," is as much for the protection of the person with time as it is for the person starting out on this journey. As she stayed sober, the pedestal she had placed me on slowly crumbled. The more available I made myself, the less she seemed to have time for me. An hour of pleasure became for me a month of pain.

Then came the day she said she would be seeing other men. Her words summoned a level of pain that had me at a breaking point.

My sponsor had assured me that sooner or later I would have to let go, and on my knees one night I begged in prayer for release from this relationship. As with my drinking, I had pursued pleasure and received pain.

Let go I did. I stopped taking her calls and quit my home group. I instructed my friends, if they wished to stay in my life, not to speak of her. In this way did I die to a dream of "reckless romancing," as Bill W. called it. My anger and hurt were intense, but, as the Big Book says, I had made a decision based on self that placed me in a position where I could be hurt.

In the years since, I have had the chance to reflect on my relationship with the opposite sex. I grew up in a female-dominated household, far too close to my mother and not close enough to an emotionally absent father. My attitudes in part were shaped by the abuse meted out by three considerably older and decidedly unhappy sisters. So it doesn't surprise me today that, the night after finding myself with a girlfriend at age 14, I was down in the park drinking a six-pack of beer with a childhood friend, the first alcohol I had ever bought. That relationship, which spanned four years, was characterized by intense obsession, as all my involvements with women were to be. I would lose my own identity in girls and later in women, and when they left, there would be nothing left of me, since they had become the thing of value. Was it any wonder that, at age 23, I should embrace alcohol, given its promise that it would be my loyal companion—unlike fickle girlfriends—and comfort and sustain me along the rocky road of life?

Many people spend their lives wondering how they can enter a relationship. My issue has been: How do I get out of them, or more accurately, how do I get to the place where I begin and they end so I don't lose myself in them?

Recently, I returned to my first home group, where I made coffee as a newcomer. I see no one from those early days at that meeting, including the well-spoken former executive whose frantic desire caught my attention on that Saturday night. I was seeing a woman in the program for a while, and we would often meet there to start our Saturday night together. But there wasn't enough to keep us together, and so, when the relationship fell away, I continued to attend that meeting. I had a primary purpose, but I also went because it had a social aspect and there were attractive women who sometimes smiled at me.

En route one week, I stopped off at a shop to have passport photos taken. "My God," I gasped inwardly, seeing not the 23-year old I am in my mind's eye but a man closer to 60 than to 50 and clearly showing his age. And so I arrived at the meeting feeling subdued and deflated and sought out a newcomer, sweaty, ill-at-ease, and lonely, and I talked with him for a while.

Whatever the future holds, I do know this. We are, as we hear over and over again, "a Fellowship of the spirit," not the body. Our minds join in common purpose when we gather in the rooms of AA. If we have to grow older, as we inevitably do, how blessed we are that we have a program along spiritual lines to guide and support us as we age. The wisest investment I can make is to continue to give myself entirely to Alcoholics Anonymous and place my life on a service basis. It is, in my experience, especially important to devote time on a daily basis to the practice of our Eleventh Step, maintaining that daily connection with the source of all life through prayer and meditation. This, it is guaranteed, will transform loneliness into aloneness, or all-oneness, in the best sense of the word.

David S.
New York, New York

A 14-Year-Old Mind in a 35-Year-Old Body
May 1999

I was seven years sober, gazing at pleasure boats streaming downriver on a warm spring afternoon, and furious that my live-in partner had confronted me with suspicions of a fling I'd had during her week's absence. Why, I thought, couldn't she just mind her own business? It had nothing to do with her. What's wrong with a short furlough now and then? I hadn't wanted her to find out; I certainly didn't want to hurt her. So live and let live, right?

In 20 years of almost daily drinking, I'd never cheated on the women I dated or the woman whom I married (and later divorced). Not even during seven of those years when I traveled as a musician for weeks at a time and had ample opportunity. I was manipulative, controlling, sometimes abusive—but not promiscuous.

I attribute this to first, parents who modeled similar behavior for better or worse (with Dad's drinking it was often for worse); and second, the peculiar tunnel vision and immaturity that alcoholism engenders. I was too fearful, insecure, childish, grandiose, and oversensitive to be sexually adventuresome.

But here I was, sober seven years and caught in the act. Good advice was available from other sober men at the time, and I ignored it. I had to find out for myself, and I paid the price.

I also learned from this event, made amends, changed my behavior, renewed my commitment, and bore the painful remorse silently for hurting two people whom I loved, and disappointing others who found out. But like my first and last drunks, my sober sexual slip is emblematic of the weird mental-emotional spin alcoholism lends to otherwise sane thinking. "Rationalization," the "Twelve and Twelve" says, "is our ancient enemy." My own mind, an enemy? Isn't it the flesh that's weak?

My sponsor often reminded me in the beginning that I had some serious growing up to do. I might look and act like a 35-year-old adult, "sane to all appearances," but when I talked about meeting women and starting a family, I sounded more like a 14-year-old boy.

Maybe watching me fall in and out of love every three months had something to do with my sponsor's opinion. But living sober and single for a few years freed me to experiment. I was going to know "a new freedom," right?

My pattern was to slip into bed by the third date. If that concluded favorably, it was a sign this woman was going to complete my life. When we reached the stage of talking about commitment, one or the other of us would express some misgivings or anger—a sure sign this relationship was less than perfect—and I'd make a hasty exit. Don't want the good to be the enemy of the best, do we?

I thought it was my sponsor's threadbare libido that prompted his advice to stay out of intimate relationships for a year and get to know myself. Regardless of how drunk and stoned, I'd never suffered the sexual dysfunction I heard other drunks talk about. Now here I was with my physical and imaginative vigor unimpaired and at full wattage all day long, week after week, and I was supposed to ignore the women around me? Their eagerness to share a little God-given creature comfort? My sponsor eventually settled for a shake of the head and a paternal reminder about using protection. He said, "Just don't drink over it, OK?"

Post-game inventories of these frequent flyers into semi-adult behavior proved me blameless, of course. Gone was my rigid adherence to "love, honor, and obey" that my parents sniped and battled through. I was honest, open, and willing to forge more equitable ground. We might have made a go of it too, if only she had acted differently. It simply wasn't meant to be. My soul-mate waited elsewhere. It was time to get on to the next one and hope for a better outcome. I could feel it. Meaning: do the same thing again, and expect different results.

So I arrived at the doorstep of my present relationship six years sober, but still clueless how to shape lasting intimacy with someone whom I genuinely loved. There's no shortage of advice in bookstores or religions about this. But ever the teenager, I relied on my own R&D.

After dating and living with a woman for two years, and genuinely enjoying a committed, sober relationship, I didn't plan the fling. In fact, I promised myself (but not my partner) that I wasn't going to do this—a pledge easily brushed aside with the rationalization that, judging by how circumstances brought the other woman and me together, our little spree had to be Higher-Powered. After all, didn't I pray every day and turn over my life and will? Who was I to turn away what God put before me?

I was disregarding two principles. 1) Just because you want to do something doesn't mean that you should. 2) As ye sow, so shall ye reap.

Confronted with the obvious, my instinct was to stonewall. It would be better for the relationship if she thought maybe my little peccadillo never happened, right? My next reaction was that it was time to get out of this relationship and get on with the next one.

Other sober alcoholics, however, reminded me that willingness was the key to working through the mess my selfish behavior had precipitated. Steps Four through Nine and couples counseling provided the tools. I'd had enough experience in asking for help and taking action by then that I trusted these were what I needed. Most important, I'd made enough mistakes to understand that maybe I couldn't rely on my own thinking.

So good was the advice and direction I received at this troubled time, that my partner and I recently celebrated 11 years together, four of them married.

A slogan I hear at meetings advises that happiness isn't found in getting everything we want, but in wanting everything we have. When I hear this I think of my marriage first, and offer a short prayer of thanks for this gift, one among many today that I cherish and honor for being beyond my understanding or deserving.

Anonymous

CHAPTER FOUR

On the Job

Learning to become a worker among workers

We spend so much of our day on the job, fielding challenge after challenge as well as the triumphs. "My place of employment for the past 25 years offers me the best opportunity to apply the principles of AA," observes Elaine L. in the story "Serenity Chair," at the same time admitting that the workplace is also where she best practices her character defects.

On the heels of what felt like a betrayal in "It Works at Work," Debra M. wisely takes a suggestion she was given at a meeting: to employ the Traditions, putting the common welfare first. On her computer during the day, she also uses such conscious login passwords as "serene" and "patience." In the story "I Almost Lost My Job—Sober," writer B.G. did picks up a drink after a period of shaky sobriety, equipping her with experience enough to list pragmatic details about what she did to secure her sobriety again.

April A.'s "Planting the Seed" is an inspiring success story about a "horrible" alcoholic coworker who's now sober and the author's dear friend. "AA can bring people together," says April, "no matter what their differences." And then there's Kelly M., the author of "The Misfit." She could never fit in at work, since the most consistent part of her resume was always her drinking career. Now sober, she knows one place where she always feels comfortable, as she heads off to her AA meeting.

It Works at Work

June 2000

A frustrating morning at work drove me to a noon AA meeting where I was called on to share. I unloaded my frustration of working with people who cared only for themselves. A coworker had (I thought) intentionally misled me about the location of a business meeting where, as a trainee, I was to observe him facilitate. This, I thought, was my big chance and he seemed intent on elbowing me out of the limelight. Four years of both college and sobriety had resulted in an unfinished degree and the title of clerk. No matter how hard I worked, nothing seemed to make a difference in either my income or my title. I was ambitious and hardworking but with no direction. I repeatedly asked my sponsor when I would know what direction I should take at work. His response was always, "Just show up and be of service."

After I concluded my whining, Joe D. was called on. He looked at me and said, "Debbie, no one was happier than I was that you worked the Steps. Now why don't you try working the Traditions? Start with the first one."

It was explained to me that to put our common welfare first, I would have to put myself second. Tradition One meant "putting ourselves to the side and working for the greater good." This was not what I expected to hear, but I had run out of ideas and became willing to try doing it differently.

It didn't take long for me to realize that in order to consider the common welfare of my work group, I had to be willing to let go of my resentments toward them, specifically toward my coworker. I had to look for my part in the situation because I knew by this time that people didn't usually avoid me without good reason. I remembered that a couple of times at a meeting which my coworker was leading, I had fired some of my sarcastic-but-funny comments at his expense. The group laughed but I remembered the look in his eyes. No wonder he was avoiding me! He couldn't control what was coming out of my mouth.

I had to clean up my side of the street with him and did so by telling him that I was both aware of and sorry for what I had done and in the future I would make every effort to support rather than embarrass him. I asked him if there was anything I could do to be of service to him. He didn't jump at my offer.

A few weeks later I saw an opportunity to be of service, and I asked him if he'd like me to assist with the design of a presentation layout for the training course he was preparing. It was an important project and one that he had put a great deal of time and effort into. He accepted my offer. This time, I had a different motive than before, designing to meet the needs of the presenter and the audience instead of my own desire to be paid more or singled out for praise. As the design began to take shape, so did my attitudes about my job. I began to experience the true satisfaction of being a worker among workers.

I found that I had an opportunity to help make something that fostered confidence rather than panic in the presenters. I even found opportunities to apply humor into the presentation, not the wicked kind that hurts but the witty kind that can help people feel good.

The week prior to the Big Event, my coworker asked me to accompany him because, as he put it, "I will have more confidence if I know you are there to help if anything goes wrong with the presentation." Imagine that.

As I worked the First Tradition to the best of my ability, I noticed a sense of well-being at work and an increased interest in others. It had never occurred to me before that the results of working the Traditions might be the same as working the Steps.

And the effect of Tradition One continues to amaze me. A few months after the Big Event, my coworker's wife entered the AA Fellowship for the first time. The combination of relief, gratitude, and awe at the power of the AA program washed over me when I realized that my behavior outside of AA could affect, either positively or negatively, a newcomer who had not yet entered our doors. What would they have thought of this program if I had not cleaned up my side of the street and worked Tradition One? Thank God we will never know because my coworker's wife liked what she saw, wanted what we had, and has just celebrated two years of sobriety. It is my privilege to be her sponsor.

What about my career and the title that I had been so anxious to attain? It comes as no surprise to me that my current job is to identify areas of need in organizations and then design information systems that will meet those needs. As for my job title, it will probably change when I complete my degree, somewhere around June 2001. Imagine that.

Debra M.
Richland, Washington

I Almost Lost My Job— Sober
August 1984

finally quit my job of 11 years the day I came to AA in 1979. Since then, I have had five jobs and that many periods of unemployment. I kept my shaky sobriety until May 3, 1982, when the pressure was so great, I picked up a drink. Usually loud and boisterous at meetings, I talked very softly at my next meeting when asking to become a part of the group again.

In the past two years, I have had to change a lot to keep my sobriety. For one thing, I prayed with a new determination, "Lord, I cannot stay sober without money to pay our bills." After resorting to food stamps during my last period of unemployment, I found another position with the agency I had worked for those 11 years. This was a last resort. I was convinced I could not hold any job if I lost this one; I had been fired and had quit so often before. Then came the clincher: We purchased a mobile home and traded cars. Both purchases were necessary. Now, I could not be so irresponsible as to quit or lose my job.

Until I got a bad reevaluation from my superiors, I did not know how close I had come to losing the job; the company has put me on three months' probation. So I have been forced to change my attitude about other people and their actions.

I had been so sure that my employers didn't appreciate me and all my hard work. I never once asked myself if I cared about my coworkers or correspondents. I was so smug, thinking I was a topnotch, efficient secretary. You will never know what it did to my ego to learn that my typing and filing were only average, that my telephone skills and inter-personal relationships were not acceptable, and that the result could be termination if my professional attitude and telephone techniques did not improve immediately.

I took a courtesy course from the phone company. I got a book from the library giving secretaries suggestions for dealing with people. And finally, I had to give God all my resentments, anger, and martyrdom on the job. You may ask what all this has to do with alcoholism. I never got along with people even before I drank a lot. And I am still an alco-holic—sober. I was not the average, normal, healthy woman before I became addicted to alcohol, and I am not now.

But I am willing to listen, learn, study, grow, and change. I have stopped competing with my coworkers and started trying to cooperate. I never wanted to be just one of the gang; I always thought of myself as better than or worse than, but always "apart from" and not "a part of." I found I must conform to others' guidelines if I wanted to stay employed. Now, I do conform.

After four years in AA, I have finally been given enough serenity to "Live and Let Live," to mind my own business, to give love and service to all my fellowmen, not just suffering alcoholics, and to practice these principles in all my affairs. No, all service and sponsoring are not done inside the AA group. I must love all people I come in contact with, for this is what my Higher Power calls me to do.

At times, life forces us to grow or die. I choose to grow through this experience, and I hope I can become a better human being for it. "We will lose interest in selfish things and gain interest in our fellows," the Big Book says. "Self-seeking will slip away. Our whole attitude and outlook upon life will change." Thank God, I found AA. Through its program, I not only became sober; I am learning to live in the world around me.

B. G.
North Little Rock, Arkansas

Serenity Chair
May 2001

My place of employment for the last 25 years offers me the best opportunity to apply the principles of Alcoholics Anonymous. I have spent more time here than anywhere else, over half my life, mostly practicing my character defects. Like anything else practiced repeatedly (it makes perfect, after all), I have gotten very good at being selfish, self-centered, full of self-pity and dishonest. It has been difficult to change in this part of my life. What I do today is try and apply the principles, the key word being try.

I have experienced growing pains in sobriety, but, gratefully, God has given me the willingness to persevere. I have gone through the Twelve Steps with a focus on my work relationships, which revealed the deep-seated feelings I bring to the table, the main one being fear. These feelings get triggered constantly throughout the day. The opposite of fear is faith, and since both cannot live in me at the same time, I practice faith and try to stay in the moment, because that is where I find my Higher Power.

I keep reminders around my desk at work, like a small picture of a chair on the beach with the first line of the Serenity Prayer, which reminds me to pray and ask for help. Inside my desk, I keep AA pamphlets, reminding me "Just for Today" and to "Let Go and Let God." I also keep a copy of the story on acceptance from the Big Book close at hand. I use program words as the passwords on my PC, such as "patience" and "serene."

Frustration and fear may always rear their ugly heads. It is what I do with them that counts. I pause when I get agitated, take some deep breaths, invite God into the situation, sit quietly, and then re-enter the moment, which I often find is now a new one.

This morning, my reading said that the best way out of a situation is through it. In my meditation, I asked God, "What is it that you are showing me at work? What is it that you want me to do?" After sitting quietly, the word that came to me was "humble." I know this had to be from my Higher Power, as this wouldn't be the word I would conjure up.

Surrender used to mean giving up or giving in. Today, it means accepting whatever is in this moment. That is my destination.

Elaine L.
South Amboy, New Jersey

The Misfit
May 2011 [Excerpt]

Never in my life have I ever really felt like the right fit.

Two weeks before Christmas, I was called into my boss's office and given the standard, "You're not a great fit and we have to let you go." Wonderful! Could this year have gotten any better?

I just could not believe this was happening. I had been with the company for four months and "not a good fit" was simply a shabby reason to be let go, especially two weeks before Christmas. This whole horrible episode happened, I believe, because I was not liked by one of the bosses and for speaking up about our hours being cut. They had sliced about $600 per month from our paychecks and I was the only one who spoke up about it. Did they just expect us to be silent and acquiesce? Of course they did. There were other reasons, I'm sure, that this happened, but nothing I could come up with seemed to assuage my broken, hurt feelings, my panic and fear or that general sickly sensation about how I could possibly celebrate the upcoming Christmas season knowing I had no job to go back to.

According to a review I had experienced less than one month before, I was doing an excellent job. This, it seemed, was the story of my life: I was not a good fit.

Never in my life have I ever really felt like the right fit. I have never had that experience of things falling into place like they are supposed to, not anywhere, not ever, not even close. I've always stood on the fringes, on the outside, looking in. To this day, I remain single while everyone around me has gotten married and had children. Things have never gone according to plan. My life has never fit into one of those neat packages wrapped up for Christmas with a lovely bow on top.

My 15-year drinking career had been the most successful career of my life, the one I had paid the most attention to. Despite being left out in the cold again by being told I was just not the right fit at this crazy job, I knew, deep down, that they were wrong. I was a great fit, just not for them. I would always fit in at AA and never had to worry about whether I would be discarded like I had just been at my former job.

It was a terrible blow when it happened. But that night, I went to a meeting and talked about my devastated feelings. I talked about how I was scared out of my skin that I would not be able to pay my bills, and how I felt, once again, like I did not fit into my life.

The difference today is that I know how to deal with feelings of not fitting in, and, with the help of my friends in AA, I know how to heal myself. By simply going to a meeting and sharing my story and the day's events with others at the meeting, I would, once again, feel like I fit.

This was not, of course, a magic answer to the real problems I was now facing:157 the loss of my income, dignity and self-respect. These problems were still there, and there was no running from them. They hurt like hell, and it was going to take some healing on my part.

I did not have to worry about who did and who did not like me when I walked into the rooms of AA, who didn't see me as a good puzzle piece. I was in a place that was immune from those kinds of judgments and I felt safe and at home.

This is still very fresh for me, a terribly disappointing and hurtful time. I still have no solutions. I still don't know when I'm going to be working again, when I will be able to feel safe and comfortable with a steady source of income.

The one thing I know is that two weeks ago, the night I was let go from my job, after I left that AA meeting, I did feel like I was a good fit. What happened to me was truly terrible, but I was not going to have to take a drink that night. For me, then and at this very moment, that's all that matters.

Kelly M.
Edmonton, Alberta

Putting Up With Mr. Bill
January 2003

There are only two of us in my department at work, Mr. Bill and I, and I wouldn't wish this coworker on anyone. He's been put in my path for a reason—only God knows why for sure. I've been letting go and letting God, praying for him almost daily, talking to my sponsor and friends, and trying to see my part in this no-win situation. Yet his behavior has had the power to dominate me.

One day, I finally lost it. My coworker is a slob, and when I asked him to pick up a vacuum hose that he had dropped and left in the middle of the floor, he merely looked at me, then at the hose by his feet. "Oh, I'll get it later," he said, and proceeded to walk over to his desk, sit down, put his feet up, and start reading a book.

I began to shake inside, with awful thoughts of causing bodily harm to this idiot running through my head. The Serenity Prayer wasn't working. In fact, prayer was the last thing on my mind at that point. This was simply another one of the many little games he plays at my emotional expense. Just pick up the damn hose!, I thought. The hose now began to grow and to take over the whole room. After two and a half years with this guy, I saw red, and was afraid of what I might do. I walked up front, tossed the keys to the building and the company vehicle to my boss's son. "I'm outta here," I said. "I don't need this job enough to put up with this jerk."

So there I was, standing in the rain on the corner, waiting for a taxi. I was almost five years sober, thinking, What the heck just happened? Now I have no job, no money, and no car to use. Who's the idiot now? Not that guy back at his workbench, chuckling at me.

I'm the type of alcoholic who manages to get through major calamities, but break a shoelace and all hell breaks loose. Well, my shoelace was that vacuum hose.

My boss called later that evening to ask what happened. I've spoken to him before about this situation with Mr. Bill, trying to get it resolved. He wishes this guy would quit, but is too nice a boss to fire him. One of the many promises in the Big Book is "you will gain the respect of others." I'm back at work with a raise and Mondays off. I've wanted long weekends for a while now. But Mr. Bill is still there.

Here's where the Serenity Prayer comes in for me. I do have the courage to change this. I'm actively applying for other jobs. I'm speaking up every time a silly situation occurs. Most importantly for me, I continue to go to meetings, and talk with my sponsor and friends. Thank God for the good and the bad. God is working in my life every second, even though I may not be able to see it. That I truly believe.

Janis H.
St. Catharines, Ontario

Planting the Seed
February 2010

worked in a department with all men. I really liked what I did, but I had my problems with some of the guys, especially one in particular—Jeff. For some reason we just did not hit it off. We never had words, he just disliked me. His attitude toward me started to manifest itself in other ways beyond just the dirty looks I would get when I walked into the room. He would take my lunch, go into my locker and mess it up, do things to my car and send me very scary messages. The things he did are too numerous to mention. I couldn't prove it was Jeff, but I knew and everyone else did, too. I took the harassment for almost two years before taking a job elsewhere on the site.

About five years after taking my new job, Jeff also came into the plant as an electrician. In my position I had to be gracious and give him what he needed to do his job. I had to use what I learned at the AA tables more than once when he came to the window. My first instinct was to slam the window in his face. This was not an option.

We managed to be civil to each other, with reserve. One day, Jeff came into the warehouse just as my coworkers and I were talking about amends. He looked at me and said, "I think I owe someone in this room an amends." I said, "Yes, you do." He apologized for his past behavior and I accepted his apology without resentment.

Two years later, Jeff was at the stockroom getting parts. I put up different quotes each week on my window, AA-related, but meaningful for everyone. He asked me where I got the quotes. I told him, "AA." Without my knowing it, a seed had been planted.

A week later Jeff asked if he could talk to me. He said, "This is none of my business, and you may not want to tell me, but are you in AA?" I told him yes, for 15 years. I could tell by the look on his face where this was going. I asked, "Do you need help?"

He said, "Yes, I do." I cannot tell you how my eyes welled up and the feeling of peace that overcame me. Jeff sat down and proceeded to tell me what his life had been like and how he was on the edge of losing all that he loved. He had not drunk since February, but was white-knuckling it the whole time. I invited him to my home group on Saturday, which meets at 7:30 A.M. daily. His desperation gave me an idea that he was serious about making life changes.

Jeff showed up that Saturday morning and started attending that meeting regularly. He now has 18 months of uninterrupted sobriety and is one of my dearest friends.

This story is a lesson on how AA can bring people together no matter what their differences. Jeff and I completed a circle from total dislike to total love and respect. All the credit goes to AA. I didn't hide that I am in recovery, and that was my gift to Jeff.

April A.
Muskegon, Michigan

The Program at Work
Grapevine Online Exclusive – January 2012

My office intercom intoned its alert that someone wanted to speak with me.

"Marc, come to my office."

"Yes, sir," I answered.

It was difficult at first because of my pride and ego, but for the last six months I had started addressing my bosses Jim and Bob as "sir." It reminded me that they were in charge and that I needed to be humble and subservient to them. This was not easy for me because of my dislike of their business practices and management styles. It also was my nature to think of myself as "the boss" and my self-centeredness was a huge part of who I was.

AA had taught me that it really wasn't any of my business to change them. They would be whoever they were going to be and I had to accept it. They were in charge and I wasn't. Additionally, I wasn't the center of the universe and I needed to learn humility. The more I learned about myself, the more I practiced the principles in all of my affairs and the more I tried to be useful to others, the more freedom and happiness I found. Calling them both "sir" was one way to do that.

I had lost the passion for my job a couple of years earlier, but continued doing it because I was good at it and it provided a good income for my family. I never gave less than 100 percent, but truthfully my heart wasn't in it.

I responded quickly to his request. As I entered his office he motioned for me to close the door and have a seat. Intuitively, I knew that this was not going to be a good conversation. The look on his face was soft and uncomfortable, not his normal demeanor.

As he began to speak about how much he disliked what he was about to do, how it was not his plan to have to do this a couple of days before the holidays and that although he had become "numb" to the process after having done over 400 of these during the last 2 years, this was the most difficult.

I knew it was coming. The company was eliminating my position and he was laying me off as of December 31. He looked distraught.

He began to explain the severance package, the separation agreement and other items, but my mind went directly to the Serenity Prayer. "God grant me the serenity to accept the things I cannot change ... " I repeated it several times in my head, not hearing a word he was saying. Suddenly I knew that this was a moment of truth. I had talked the talk of Alcoholics Anonymous, but this challenge would prove if I could truly walk the walk.

I looked at Jim and I knew I had to comfort him; I had to show him love. What I have learned in the past four years and what I have tried to become ... it happened. No thoughts of drinking, no resentment, no plans of vengeance.

Resentments are my biggest hurdle and unless I forgive, I cannot be forgiven. As long as the anger, fear and guilt of my resentments occupy space in my mind they own me. I have to comfort and understand those I am resentful toward and accept my part in it. Then and only then will I experience the freedom and joy of life that I am seeking. If I treat everyone with love, admiration and respect, my life will be without resentments. One day at a time.

I told him how much I appreciated what he had done for me, how blessed I felt to have been able to keep my job during the last two years, and asked if there was anything I could do to make this transition easier for him. The more love I showed him, the more he offered to include in my severance package. At one point he said that there was a week left in my paid vacation benefit and he would make sure I got it. I told him I had used up all my vacation benefits; he stopped me and said he was sure I had another week coming.

Normally, I would have been angry. My resentment would have kept me from being level-headed. But everything I have learned in my recovery worked, because I worked it.

I feel blessed. I now have a chance to start the new career I have been wanting. I am not sure what it will be, but God knows and that is all that matters.

Marc D.

It Works at Work (If You Work It)
December 2000

've been sober for a little more than three years, and each year (heck, each month) of sobriety makes it clearer and clearer how little I know about living life on life's terms. But it's also clearer and clearer that I don't have to do it alone; I have a basis for living in the program of Alcoholics Anonymous. I feel as though each year sober I gain about seven years of emotional growth, so at age 50 I'm taking on life as a college-aged woman, and if I'm still sober at age 70, emotionally I'll be 141 years old! My first sponsor used to say I think too much, and I guess that still holds true. My mind runs like a horse that's escaped its corral. But I'm in the process of recreating myself, which is tricky any way you look at it, but trickier around people who knew me "when" and don't know where I'm coming from now, since I choose to remain anonymous.

So here I am, growing along emotional and spiritual lines, going to work 40 hours a week with people who are insecure, back-stabbing, and control-seeking. In other words, people just like me—except that I now have a program that suggests such things as taking a daily inventory, turning my life and my will over to my Higher Power and promptly admitting when I'm wrong, and avoiding gossip. I've worked with these people for 10 years, and for seven of them I was in the thick of every nasty bit of slanderous, back-stabbing event. So, how do I survive now? Do I throw their defects in their faces and stand superior, waving my new insight aloft like a banner? Do I withdraw from all personal conversations and take all my breaks alone, hiding in the bathroom or in my car? By relating her difficulties working with personalities who weren't in a program, my sponsor has helped me realize that being superior and unavailable isn't the best or the only alternative.

Tradition One has kept me from going off the deep end at work. In the section about Tradition One, the "Twelve and Twelve" says that we realize we are but a small part of a great whole, that it becomes plain that the group must survive or the individual will not, and that the struggle for wealth, power, and prestige tears humanity apart. Of course, this refers to us alcoholics. But when I apply it to my workplace, I can find some measure of peace in a stress-filled, dysfunctional environment.

First, when I refrain from seeing myself as the center of the universe and see myself as just one more person showing up to earn wages to survive, my ego deflates and I don't need to get embroiled in the latest gossip or even be liked in order to feel safe. Second, when I realize that without these other people, or another group just like them, the company wouldn't exist, I appreciate the job I have and accept that working with others is just a fact of life unless I want to work security on the graveyard shift at a cemetery. Third, when I watch others vie for morsels of power, haggle and complain about wages, and use passive-aggressive behavior, I can see it for what it is: sad and pathetic. Seeing that allows me to feel gratitude that I don't have to go there with them.

I am not a saint. It's a struggle to stay not just in the game but above the fray, and sometimes I slip. I always feel disappointed in myself afterward until I make an amends. Then I get right with my Higher Power, by admitting my defects and turning them over once again, knowing that I'm OK as long as I'm working from the heart. However, by applying the message found in Tradition One to my workplace, I can find a relative amount of sanity. All I have to do is keep sight of the bigger picture, keep my ego right-sized, and appreciate the fact that people in other positions allow the company to function and me to earn the wages I need to survive.

I use Tradition One when interacting with family, too, but that's another story. What I was like before sobriety was desperate. What I'm like today is hopeful and willing. For this, I thank my Higher Power and the program of Alcoholics Anonymous, which has provided me with fellowship and the tools for living a sober and spiritually-based life.

Lori B.

Glendora, California

Payback Time

April 2007

I n early sobriety, I had troubles with my family, creditors, friends, and even God. But I always found a way to work through them using the tools of AA. Then, when I had been sober for nearly seven years, I suddenly encountered trouble at my place of employment. The time for my annual review came around, and I was looking forward to an increase in pay and a healthy pat on the back. Instead, the review was so bad that I wound up on probation for 90 days and was warned that if my performance did not improve during that time, I would be terminated. I had always gotten great reviews and was not ready for this. I was devastated because my job had been the only solid ground I stood on throughout my sobriety.

The problem, I realized, actually began way back in my drinking days. The person who wrote my bad review was someone I'd had a resentment against from the first time I worked with him. Although I was an experienced person in my field, I'd had to ride along with him the first week to learn how the company expected things to be done. He was not friendly and went out of his way to make things hard on me. The last day I rode with him, he left me stranded in a place that I was not familiar with, and it took me hours to find my way back to the office. I never forgot this, and there was never any love lost between us. Eventually, my drinking caused me to lose this job and I moved back to my home state, where I thought things would be better.

I went through another five years of drinking and losing jobs until April 1990, when I had my last drink. I had become unemployable, not because my workmanship was bad, but because no one wanted the baggage that came with employing a drunk.

In need of a job, I called my old employer and said that I'd been sober a year and a half. I lied. It had only been three months. The people there hired me back, and I did my last geographical. The company was very kind to me and gave me all the help they could. I worked very hard to be a good employee, trying to make amends by being an asset to them.

I was very grateful, and things went well for a long time. I was promoted to a position where I had power over my old enemy, and I used it to back charge his pay. I never extended any grace to him as I did to others for the same errors. I even got him suspended without pay once, all legitimate, but I could have handled it differently. This fellow was in every Fourth Step I ever did, but I was unwilling to let go of my resentment and clear my side of the street.

The day came when he was promoted to a position over me. The Big Book states, "Driven by a hundred forms of fear, self-delusion, self-seeking, and self-pity, we step on the toes of our fellows and they retaliate. Sometimes they hurt us, seemingly without provocation, but we invariably find that at some time in the past we have made decisions based on self which later placed us in a position to be hurt." Retaliate he did, with the worst review I have ever received!

At first, I was very angry—the fear of losing my livelihood was upsetting. So, I called my sponsor and told him what was going on. He suggested that I do an inventory on my job performance and I did, trying to be as fearless and as searching as I could, like the Fourth Step suggests. I then took my inventory and compared it to my supervisor's review, identifying the areas where he was right and resolving to improve in those areas. In the areas where I felt he was wrong, I decided to do nothing.

The 90 days passed and it was time for my second review. This time it was worse than the first, and the C.E.O. of our company attended. AA has taught me to "right size" myself in all things, and I have learned that there are times when I should stand up for myself and times when I should defer. So, I was able to point out to the C.E.O. that the detrimental items in the second review were all different from those in the first. In fact, the second review noted that I had improved on all of the questionable areas in the first review. The C.E.O. said he thought maybe a personality conflict was the problem, and he would research it. We would meet again in one week.

A week passed and now I had a third review to go over. I was ready to go to war, if I had to. The night before, I prayed about this, asking God to do his will and to allow me the grace to accept the outcome, no matter how it worked out.

My third review was a very good one, with a nice raise. The C.E.O. told my supervisor and me that we were both valuable to the company and that we should work out our differences. I sat there, still ready to argue my point. Then a reassuring voice welled up inside me and said, "Let it go." I know it was my Higher Power working on me. I thanked them both and walked out of the office.

From that point on, my supervisor and I did work out our differences. We worked well together. When a few years later he was terminated, I actually felt sympathy for him—imagine that! I learned again that if I look for the answers in the Twelve Steps and God there is a solution to every problem that I might face in life. My old drinking self would have run away or come up with a "non-solution" to this problem. By asking God, my sponsor, and a host of AAs for help, I got to face my problem with professionalism and poise. Later I was able to leave the job with dignity and pride, and today I own my own company.

The program of Alcoholics Anonymous solved the biggest problem in my life—alcohol. I have come to learn that everything else is small change.

Steve V.

Gold Canyon, Arizona

CHAPTER FIVE

Friendship

Satisfying, lasting relationships are counted
among the Fellowship's great gifts

" was a loner all my life," begins Jim D.'s "A Circle of Friendship," this chapter's first story, setting a familiar AA theme for this section on friendship. In families, in marriages, in crowds, even at parties, an inexplicable loneliness always seems to haunt active alcoholics. The remedy is our custom-made Fellowship. These stories make it clear that our meetings offer us more people of honesty and courage than we found in a lifetime of drinking, when our friendships were as unmanageable as the rest of our lives.

In the stories "Listening to Walter" and "Friends for Life," we discover sober instruction manuals for developing the extraordinary yet simple qualities that make time-tested friendships available, even inevitable.

In "Garage Opener," an open door only becomes an open invitation when Clardy S. finds the courage to walk in. From the stunning synchronicities of "The Cheetah and His Bubba," by Floyd K., to the clarifying observations of Rick R.'s "Real Friends," the stories in this chapter remind us that AA bonds are as satisfyingly deep as they often are because they connect survivors of the same sinking ship.

A Circle of Friends

December 1992

was a loner all my life. I was always scared and ashamed. I was poor, I lived in a dilapidated house, and my alcoholic father put my family through hell. I never had any friends. I despised alcohol for dealing me such a rotten break in life.

As an adult, I vowed never to be poor again, and succeeded. But I fell to alcohol, like my father, and those fears of people, places, and things never left me. I made several geographical moves, hoping to magically fit into society with a new start. They never worked.

When I finally walked through the doors of AA, people smiled and introduced themselves to me. They sensed that I wanted terribly to get sober, but didn't know how to ask for help. So some of them hugged me and told me that they loved me, and asked me to keep coming back. They loved me unconditionally. My new friends listened to me and cared about me. They also trusted me and brought out the hidden qualities in me. In return, they asked nothing from me. No one cared about my past, where I lived, or where I worked.

When I was six months sober, while I was in a shopping mall with one of my daughters, I ran into a fellow AA named Fred. Fred got a big smile on his face. He went on and on about how happy he was to see me. He introduced himself to my 10-year-old daughter and made a big deal over meeting her, too. Fred told my daughter that I was a good man.

After Fred went his way, my daughter asked me who he was. I said, "He's my friend." She shocked me with her reply: "Quit kidding, Daddy, who is he really? You don't have any friends."

Her innocent statement hurt for a moment. But then I realized it wasn't true anymore. For the first time in my life I really did have friends. I have even more friends today. Together we share our experiences, strengths, and hopes. I don't know the last names of many of my friends or what they do for a living. I do, however, extend the same unconditional love to them which was so freely given to me. I look forward to attending meetings so I can be with my friends.

I still get tears in my eyes when people in AA introduce me to others as their friend.

Jim D.

Columbus, Ohio

Where Everybody Knows My Name

October 2010

grew up watching a lot of TV sitcoms, and recall "All in the Family," where Archie Bunker sat for hours in his chair saying, "Shut up, Edith, and get me a beer." I also remember the show "Cheers," where everyone hollered out "Norm!" and the theme song about "Where everybody knows your name, where they're always glad you came." Truthfully, I always loved that feeling of walking into a bar, having the bartender pour my beverage of choice, and people chiming out my name, welcoming me home.

My story is not a scripted show with built-in laugh tracks, but it is truly a reality show. Most of my family was out of state, so as a hardworking single woman, loneliness was one of the things that led to my drinking more. It was also one of the things that I struggled with as I began my sobriety, letting go of many friends and activities that had come to define my very existence. Yet as I write, I realize that I'm beginning to have a new home.

I will always remember the Friday night I came to my first AA meeting. I had called an AA-related clubhouse earlier to find out about meeting times. When I walked in that evening, I must have had the deer in the headlights look of the newbie, because someone quickly invited me to sit at the counter and have a cup of coffee before the meeting started. Another guy got a packet of pamphlets and a phone list together for me. I walked into the meeting and tried to pick up on the conversations and the jargon in the room. There seemed to be several people speaking at different times. "Twelve Steps" I'd heard of. "Twelve Promises"? Not a clue. "How It Works"? Totally foreign, and it didn't explain anything just then.

I quickly realized that there were many rituals involved with the meetings and I'd just have to watch and figure it out. They went around the room introducing themselves and when it came to me, I sobbed, "I'm Jill and I'm an alcoholic," choking on every word as it came out of my mouth.

Flash forward to another meeting. I came to the Saturday morning meeting feeling a bit befuddled. I had just celebrated my fifth month of sobriety and my bellybutton birthday earlier in the week, and was contrasting how great it was to have a sober birthday framed by morning and evening meetings in contrast to the year before when I'd started with Bloody Marys in the morning, drinks with lunch, wine with a pedicure, dinner and drinks, a few birthday shots and then on to a night of karaoke and booze. Yes, I was feeling good about my newfound sobriety, and beginning to feel secure in it. I was also cleaning my house in other ways.

But this week, three people I knew from the club had relapsed. I began thinking about the people I had seen come in and out the door in this short period of time. This scared the heck out of me. How would I protect my own sobriety? I did not want to become a relapse statistic. As one of the guys was fond of saying, "I know I have another drunk in me, but I don't know if I have another recovery."

This particular meeting had a topic of "Here and Now." The second woman to speak had been sober about two weeks, and her sharing changed the focus of the meeting. Many of the participants directed their stories and their memories toward our newest member.

I saw a number of AA friends that I hadn't seen for a couple of weeks, and was really excited to be with the group. There were also a number of old-timers there, and they were having a good time giving each other grief. But they were also passing along tremendous wisdom. One man with many years of sobriety said to the newcomer, "Don't just come to the meetings, but come to the club, come to the dances, get involved with the people and the activities. Let them become your friends. I met my wife here and we celebrated our 26th anniversary this year."

Another old-timer spoke of the need to allow his Higher Power to be a part of the program, and how he'd been in AA forever, but continued to relapse until he could turn it over to God. The next gentleman said, "I never learned to read very well, but I learned to listen. I listen to audiotapes and CDs from the Big Book, from Grapevine and from meetings and speakers." He concluded with his favorite line, "You've got to take the cotton out of your ears and put it in your mouth and listen."

The next old-timer razzed the first one for being in the program "200 years" and the group laughed, but then he talked about what those fellows had been through over the last three decades, and how important it is to listen. "Listen to your sponsor, your peers and all the wisdom that is within. While everybody's story may have some unique elements, there are also those elements that are universal. That's why we nod in agreement, in empathy, in understanding. And remember to watch their faces as you listen. You will learn much."

The words he spoke to our newcomer went right to my heart, as I was struggling with work on my Fourth Step. "There is nothing you can do, nothing you can say, that somebody here hasn't already done. You can't shock us. We are here, and we will love you, encourage you, support you and kick your butt when you need it. All you have to do is want to be sober. All you have to do is not take the first drink." As I write now, recalling that meeting, I realize that nothing I am sharing here is really different than what you will hear at any meeting. Rather it was all the good, simple AA wisdom combined. But that is the beauty of AA. Some way, somehow, every meeting I go to seems to have exactly what I need to hear that day and a profound sense of wisdom pervades it.

What a wonderful motley crew, what a wonderful family in sobriety. It struck me then that AA has been around since 1935, and is celebrating its 75th anniversary, but in this room alone there was the collective wisdom and insights of well more than 150 years of sobriety! I've been in the program five months, and already feel so attached to these people, their stories, and their journeys. I have already gone to funerals of family members. I go to lunch with girlfriends, and nod when I see a fellow from AA at church or the local coffee shop. There is no longer a sense of embarrassment at being "one of them."

Just like any big family, we can drive each other nuts once in a while. That's why it is good to go to other meetings at different locations, but I always come home to my family at this club and the variety of the meetings held there. Here, I know someone will notice when I've not been at a meeting in a few days and call and see how it's going, or welcome me back with a question of, "Are you doing OK?" There I know Jeannie or Kris or Beth or Karen will call to see if I need a ride to a meeting. Betty will pull out an energy drink for me when she sees me walk in the door toward the counter. There I know Terry will always tease me for walking in late, Jeff will be at the counter to shout "Jilly-bean" when I walk in, Ron will hand me a root beer candy, and as I sit next to my friend Jill in a meeting she will say, "I'm Jill and I'm an alcoholic," and I will look at her and say, "No, I'm Jill and I'm an alcoholic," and we will all laugh. And with that, I pass.

Jill M.
West Bend, Wisconsin

Listening to Walter
August 2010

met my friend Walter one Christmas Day when I took my children to a nursing home to do service work. They walked around with me, passing out decks of playing cards, pairs of socks and sugar-free candies. We passed a table where a man in a wheelchair was talking to a friend. I heard him say something about "the Big Book" and "the Steps," so I stopped and asked if he was a friend of Bill W. He was. I introduced myself and he told me he'd been sober for about 25 years. He couldn't get to meetings much anymore because he was in this home, stuck in a wheelchair. It was hard for him to get around, so I offered to bring a meeting to him.

Once a month, I'd visit Walter in the nursing home for a Big Book study. Sometimes a friend or two would join us, but mostly it was just me and Walter talking program. If I couldn't go, one of my sponsees went in my place. I had been sober for a while by then, but I learned a lot about recovery listening to Walter's stories. It turned out, by the way, that the conversation I'd overheard on Christmas Day was the first time he'd spoken about recovery to anyone at that nursing home.

A few years later, I moved away and Walter changed homes. We lost touch for six months, but he found me again right around Christmas. My husband and I had just separated, my sponsor was out of the country, and I was having a very hard time. I'd put the kids in bed around nine, then wash dishes and straighten the house. At 10, when my work was done, the fears would rush in. That was when the phone would ring. It would be Walter, calling to say hi. I don't know how he knew exactly when to call, but that voice on the phone got me out of my fears and back into grace. We'd talk about the weather. He'd tell stories about his childhood in the South. He told me about the jobs he'd held. And we talked about recovery.

Walter was almost 70 when I met him and he still referred to his parents as "Mama and Daddy." My father has never talked to me as much as Walter did. Even when we have the opportunity, he's too busy, too distracted. Walter took time to listen to what was going on in my life. When he had experience, strength and hope to share, he shared it. When he didn't have a clue, he reminded me to turn it over to God.

Over the years, there were times when I needed Walter's help and times when he needed mine. At one point, he moved into a nursing home nearby. Helping him move in, getting his furniture there and picking up his groceries got me through the first summer my children spent away from me. That summer, I even found a way to get him to a real AA meeting at my home group and we went out to breakfast with some of my friends afterward. He'd thank me for helping him. I don't think he really knew how much he helped me.

Walter died a year ago, and I had the privilege of attending a memorial service for him and meeting the friends and family members I'd heard so much about through his stories. Among his belongings, we found all of his AA coins rolled up in paper like a stack of silver dollars. Everybody took one to remember him by. I've got his 15-year coin on my keychain, where it's been since my anniversary last spring. I think of him every time I see it.

A. D.
Texas

Garage Opener
March 2009

I t all started about five years ago. I was attending 7 A.M. meetings "on the porch" in Jupiter, next to the lighthouse. I began to notice a fellow who looked a bit uncomfortable and really didn't say much. One day, we had a short conversation; then later, another.

As it turned out, we were neighbors and lived only a few blocks from each other. During one of our conversations, Michael mentioned he would, at times, sit in his garage at night with the door up, smoking a cigar. This was after the kids were in bed, usually past 9 P.M. Here Michael would sit alone and contemplate how his sober life was progressing. Since I occasionally smoked a cigar, I sort of invited myself over. Michael said it was OK; I don't think he thought I would ever show.

One night a few weeks later, at about 9:15 P.M., I drove over to see if Michael was up. He was sitting in the dark—garage door up, cigar smoke billowing out—pondering important matters. After the surprise left his face, he offered me a stogie and we smoked and talked.

This was the beginning of a friendship that has grown over the years. Michael, like me and many others in AA, really didn't have many friends to talk to and share life experiences with. Sometimes we would talk for hours. I later met Michael's wife, son and daughter.

During the next few months, Michael and I talked and smoked and became good friends. He opened up at meetings but still had a hard time reaching out to others. Something about being different, as I recall, and the spirituality part of the program didn't sit too well with him. "Welcome to the club," I would say. "Many of us struggled with spirituality in the beginning."

One day Michael announced that he was moving away, taking a new job in Maryland. The telephone became a major factor in our friendship. He didn't think much of that idea. The "100-pound phone" played a part in my life earlier in sobriety, so I knew how difficult it was to get into the habit of calling, and also how rewarding it could be. I mentioned to Michael how I remained in telephone contact with an old AA friend from Houston for more than 15 years and we spoke almost monthly.

Every fall I travel to Maryland on business, and I always plan to spend time with Michael and his family. Michael and I usually take a long walk in the beautiful woods behind his new home and have in-depth conversations about the program, spirituality and how much we have to be grateful for. We all have issues to deal with. Along the way, I have learned that life is not so much what happens to us but how we are able to deal with it, and that with good communication with our Higher Power we can handle anything. Prayer and meditation are essential.

"To watch people recover, to see them help others, to watch loneliness vanish, to see a Fellowship grow up about you, to have a host of friends—this is an experience not to be missed."

I used to think that a 7 A.M. meeting was an early time to start the day. Michael's new morning meeting is at 6 A.M.—now that's really early—but I went with him anyway and met his new AA friends and the person who was to become his sponsor. The camaraderie available to us in this program is truly amazing—friendships so valuable, ones we have never had before.

But why are they important? If you know what it's like to be lonely and not have one true friend, then you understand. The loneliness of an alcoholic is like no other. To have a friend, we must be a friend. Michael now has a calling—to be a friend to someone who has none, to show the next man the way.

It will soon be fall once again and time for me to be sitting on Michael's back porch, puffing on a cigar and sharing my life with a friend, a friend that Alcoholics Anonymous has given me.

Clardy S.
Port St. Lucie, Florida

The Cheetah and His Bubba

June 2000

The Cheetah slept on my living room couch, exhausted after a full day outdoors. I sat on the floor with my back resting against the fireplace and admired Cheetah's lean youthful limbs, watching his breathing, tracking Cheetah's dollar store sunglasses as they slid downward with each deep breath toward the tip of his sunburned nose.

"My nickname is Cheetah," he had revealed to me just before dropping off to sleep. "My real name is Zackariah but they call me Cheetah because I can run very fast." He needn't have told me. We had spent a sunny day together, eating in fast food restaurants, running across playgrounds, and hiking through the woods, and by the time evening fell I was far more tired than he was. In fact I was dog-tired. After all, a 60-year-old man is absolutely no match for a 6-year-old child. But in a few days I'd be eager and ready to do it all over again! You see, I am Zackariah's lifelong friend.

His presence in my life represents the fulfillment of an AA promise. A friend had predicted this one night at the Northwest Alano Club just outside Detroit, where I used to meet with my home group. "If you can continue to stay sober," he promised me, "then you will once again experience things that you thought were gone forever."

He was of course referring to family. I was divorced and living alone. My surviving children had all flown the nest to raise families of their own. At my age it surely looked as though the golden family days of little league baseball and matinee movies and picnics at the beach were a thing of the past. This represented a grave loss. Like most other men, I badly needed my own "special place," a respected niche among those I love.

It was at this point in my life when Zack's mother phoned me from a hospital maternity room one winter morning. With her husband sitting at her bedside, she said, "I called to tell you that there's three of us now. We have a healthy baby boy. He'll be home tomorrow. We want you to come over to the house and meet him. His name is Zackariah."

I readily accepted their invitation and drove to Zack's house the next afternoon. As I sat in a rocking chair and for the first time held him in my arms, I unexpectedly discovered a lump in my throat and something in my eye. At that moment my life took a turn. Zack and I bonded. We have been close friends ever since.

We have shared many an adventure over the years. Our early exploits involved green beans and grape jelly toast eaten from a teetering high chair. A few years down the road I found myself building skyscrapers out of wooden blocks and watching a 3-year-old's giant laugh while he kicked them apart.

Today our days together pass swiftly, filled with swings and slides, backyard swimming pools and beaches, movie matinees, two-wheel bicycles with wobbly training wheels, quick trips to the town dollar store to purchase a pair of cheap sunglasses, winter evenings sharing television cartoons, and the myriad other joys I had thought were gone forever, due in part to my lack of faith and an alcoholic past.

Eleven years ago I entered Alcoholics Anonymous as a drunken agnostic. Ninety meetings in 90 days planted a spiritual mustard seed which took root and blooms today. Early on in recovery I began noticing "all those little coincidences" the old-timers used to talk about, coincidences so numerous as to defy pure chance and point instead to the presence of a Higher Power.

One such major coincidence occurred shortly after Zack's mother, who was among my closest friends, married his father. Before his birth they lived far away from me on the other side of town. They later moved to old Warrendale on Detroit's West Side and, through a remarkable coincidence, bought a starter home two blocks away from the very house where I grew up.

That day when I went to meet Zack for the first time, I was intrigued to find myself taking a nostalgic drive down the streets where I had played kick-the-can and touch football as a kid. From that day forward, I intuitively began to consider the possibility that Zack's mother had been placed into my life by a Higher Power who knew that our friendship would help me grow spiritually. This intuition has proven correct.

Zack's mother and father are deeply spiritual people. Through them and their wonderful son, the Cheetah, I am once again able to delight in those joys which I thought had vanished forever from my life. As my Big Book promises at the bottom of page 83, I am experiencing "a new freedom and a new happiness," and I am realizing that God is doing for me what I could not do for myself. Today I neither regret the past nor wish to shut the door on it.

To the contrary, with Zack I am able to relive those "golden days" I thought were gone forever and, in the bargain, revisit the wonders of my own early childhood. Today I even have a new name. My close friends call me "Bubba." Cheetah bestowed this title upon me when he was an 18-month-old toddler.

The AA promises are clearly being fulfilled in my life, sometimes slowly, sometimes quickly. All I need do is work for them. It is very important that I labor diligently, one day at a time, to remain sober.

I want to be worthy of my name.

Floyd K.
Kingsford, Michigan

More Fun Than TV
August 2003

My first year in AA, I'd end the work week by attending a meeting, then go home and watch "The Love Boat" and "Fantasy Island." Man, was that depressing!

I was 22 years old, trying my best to avoid the people, places and things of my addiction ... but there *had* to be a better way. Those nights watching the cruise ship in Puerto Vallarta and Ricardo Montalban were some of the loneliest of my life, and I knew I would eventually drink.

I finally started to meet people by going to AA early and setting up chairs and cleaning ashtrays afterward. (Those were the days when we smoked at most meetings.) One week, some young people asked me to go out for ice cream. I was thrilled! This was a far cry from the wild, high-risk life of alcoholism, but it sure beat sitting home alone.

Slowly our little gathering of young people, all in early recovery, took on a life of its own. One night, I cooked a spaghetti dinner after a meeting. Next, we started going to AA-sponsored dances together; there was strength in numbers, and it was much more comfortable walking in as a group. Then there were AA-sponsored hayrides, pool parties, and breakfasts. Suddenly I had something fun to do almost every weekend.

As we each celebrated AA anniversaries, our outings and social life broadened to include day trips to the beach and weekends at rented cabins in the mountains. Some of these excursions included AA meetings, some included discussions of Twelve Step issues, and others were simply times of fellowship and sobriety. Some of the best nights were just renting videos and hanging out together.

One of my favorite things, which I thought I'd lost forever, was the thrill and excitement of going to concerts. We learned that this was just another hurdle to overcome together. Our group went to a few concerts, always with a sobriety "game plan." We always brought more than one car, so if anyone got uncomfortable he or she could leave.

My friends and I had great times those first few years. I know in my heart that this fellowship and fun helped keep me in the program. As I struggled through the heartbreak and regret of my alcoholism, as I battled many demons in my Fourth Step, as I white-knuckled it through job and family life, those fun times were my oasis. I was making real friends, laughing a lot, enjoying good music, great food, new experiences, all while staying sober!

All these years later, my fun now revolves around my young children, church, and family. It is different, but it is all built on that solid AA foundation and fellowship that took me away from the lonely land of television.

Maria M.

Delaware

Friends for Life
January 1993

" met my husband in the looney bin. I was suicidal and he was alcoholic."

I didn't know what to make of my new friend. This was only our third visit together, and I had asked where she met her husband. It seemed like a safe enough, get-to-know-you type of question. Now we were sitting at her kitchen table, and she was telling me about her time in a mental institution. I wasn't shocked that she'd been in the "looney bin." The psychiatrist my parents had taken me to when I was 14 wanted to put me in one, and now 10 years later, I felt like I belonged in one for sure. What shocked me was the matter-of-fact way she told me. She wasn't ashamed or elusive about it. She just told me "what she used to be like and what happened." I knew I wanted to hear more from this woman.

As we spent time together around other people, I learned that Pat was the same with them, no matter who they were or how well she knew them. It was fun to go places with her and watch how people reacted to her. Not that she was loud or boisterous or volunteered a lot of unsolicited information about herself. In fact, she didn't talk about herself much at all, but when a topic came up, she didn't shirk it, and people were drawn to her. The variety of folks who might be at her house any time I dropped in never ceased to amaze me, and she was able to draw us all together with no effort at all.

I had moved to Pat's town a few months before as part of my latest "geographical cure." I was living on a ranch with several other people who, like me, were trying to "get their heads together." A few had been placed there by the courts as an alternative to jail. Most of us had been abusing alcohol and other drugs for several years, and were looking for something better (whether we knew it or not at the time). I had a car and several of them didn't, so when it came time for them to attend their court-ordered AA meetings, they asked me for a ride into town. I thought I'd satisfy my curiosity and attend a few open meetings with them. I was impressed and almost wished that my drinking was "bad enough" for me to fit in this group of people. We always hit the bar as soon as the meeting was over, but I didn't stop thinking about what I'd seen and heard.

I had gotten to know Pat informally around town, and since she was an active Al-Anon member, we had talked some about AA. I'd go to Pat with questions, and her house became my haven, away from all the madness I was involved in. She started teaching me about "one day at a time" long before I got sober. Once, for example, I cried on her shoulder when I thought I was pregnant. I wasn't married and I was scared. She listened very attentively, so I continued the list of woes—even down to the fact that my house was an absolute pig sty, and I was too paralyzed by depression to do anything about it. Finally she kind of summarized the whole situation in a way that told me she had really heard me. And then she pointed out that there was nothing I could do about it that day if I was pregnant, and nothing I could do that day about a lot of other things, but I could do my dishes, and with that thought she sent me home. I remember thinking how cold it was of her to send me home to do my dishes when my world was falling apart. But I did them, and she was right. I had done the one thing I could do that day, and I felt better. To this day, when I'm facing some problem or dilemma, I think of Pat and ask myself, "What can I do about it today?" Usually there is some action I can take—however small or insignificant—and if there isn't it's easier to apply the Serenity Prayer once I've put it in that perspective.

Pat could say things to me about my chemical use that other people couldn't, I suppose because I knew that she'd love me whether I ever quit or not. She used to tell me, "When you decide you're ready, just give me a call. I'll fill up the car with gas, and we'll haul you off to treatment."

She had a 17-year-old son named Mike who'd already been through treatment once, and she had told him that if he chose to get high, he couldn't live in their home. Mike and I were getting high and drunk together on a regular basis. Sometimes Pat would confide in me about her concerns for him, and her suspicions that he was using, and I'd sit there and pretend to be a supportive, concerned friend, when in fact Mike had been over to my house the evening before. About a month before I went to treatment, someone broke into my house and stole my marijuana. When I got home and found out my house had been broken into, I called the police (I didn't mention the missing marijuana, of course). They followed tracks from my window to Mike's house, and then I had to decide whether or not to press charges. I talked to Pat about my "quandary," because I was really mad at Mike, and in my delusion and self-righteousness I thought it might "do Mike good to suffer the consequences of his actions." She listened quietly to all my high and mighty talk about her son. It took me two years of sobriety to make amends to her about that, because I was so afraid that I'd lose her friendship. When I did, she told me she'd known that all along and had forgiven me long ago.

Pat could help me correct my perspective with a few words. At my first AA birthday celebration, I'd gotten a lot of cards and congratulations, and people said nice things about me, and I was flying high. After the meeting, she gave me a hug and said, "So, are you going to go for another 24 hours?"

After I'd been sober for 18 months, I found out I had cancer. I asked Pat to go with me to a brain scan I was scheduled for the next day. She agreed and said, "What does one wear to a brain scan, anyway?" She spent the entire day at the hospital when I had my surgery, and held my pan when I vomited. When I came out of the anesthesia and tried to talk to her, she insisted that she wasn't there to be entertained, and that I should just rest.

Pat was one of the first people I'd been around for a long time who made a relationship with God look like something I wanted. And I'd been around a lot of church folks. She showed me about a God of love, instead of one with a bunch of rules and a hammer to use on me when I screwed up.

It wasn't all serious, though. We had some great times together. We made fudge and cookies in her kitchen, went camping and shopping. She introduced me to the man who later became my husband. Once when the four of us were in a mall, Pat and I saw some cheap earrings we both liked. I bought us each a pair, and when I handed Pat hers and was going to put mine in my purse and throw away the sack, I did it backwards and threw away the earrings by mistake. I was going to leave them there (they were only a dollar) but Pat didn't give it a second thought. Next thing I knew she had the lid off the trash can and was digging through it. Our husbands stood off at a distance like they didn't know us, and later said we looked like a couple of hungry bag ladies. We finally found the earrings at the bottom and put all the trash back in. When we started to walk away, we looked up and saw that we had drawn quite a crowd.

Pat died several years ago of cancer. She used to keep a Bible verse above her kitchen sink in every house she lived in, and it was what she prayed that her life would be like. It said, "The Lord God has given me the tongue of discipline, that I may know how to sustain the weary one with a word." When I looked around at her funeral and saw other people who, like me, were alive largely because of Pat's influence in their lives, I knew he had answered her prayer.

Anonymous
Holdrege, Nebraska

Winning Friends

March 2002

When I got sober, I liked the fellowship of AA—the social interaction that happened naturally when I saw the same people every week at a meeting. But I was still solitary. While I was close to my sponsor, it was mostly based on AA, working the Steps, and making the occasional Twelfth Step call. My old ideas, my old perspectives, my defense mechanisms, my lack of trust led me to be alone most of the time. I included others only to the extent that I had to in order to get by.

After six years of sobriety, during a Fifth Step discussion, my sponsor asked me, "Do you have any friends?" I replied automatically, "Of course." As we talked, I realized that I had some acquaintances, and some were closer than others, but very few close friends.

My sponsor gave me some homework. He told me to look around in my meetings and select four or five people whom I liked and then pursue them as friends. We talked about what that meant. We agreed that for me to have close friends, I would have to open myself up to these folks, and go out of my way to see them on a regular basis. I would have to look for ways to concern myself with them and not just myself. I suppose that nonalcoholic people might find this process extremely elementary, perhaps childlike. But again and again, I find that I've learned basic living skills from my experience in Alcoholics Anonymous.

During my second and third year of sobriety, I had begun an exercise program and had taken an interest in hiking, jogging, cross-country skiing, and other outdoor activities. I used these interests as the basis for approaching my new prospects. In conversations with them, I mentioned my interests and suggested that we share a hike or a 5K race. In addition, I called them occasionally and we would go to lunch.

What a surprise! Soon I had two friends! We jogged together. We hiked together. I would drop by the shop of one and visit when I was out and about doing my work. We shared weekday lunches on occasion. We also shared on that intimate level that AA members share. Over a period of a few years, my new friendships blossomed into valuable, life-sustaining relationships. Today, I can't imagine doing without friends. I can't imagine how I maintained my solitary existence for so long.

After some time, I moved several thousand miles away for a job opportunity. It was two years before I returned to the Southwest, to settle some 400 miles from my old friends. Since my return, we've established two events we participate in without fail every year. We get together on Memorial Day weekend at a beautiful rustic campsite halfway between our homes. In October, we backpack into the Superstition Mountain Wilderness in Arizona. These two events have become the high points of my year. We have enjoyed perhaps six Memorial Day campouts, and as many as 12 or 13 Superstition Mountain backpacks.

In addition, with my newfound friend-finding skill, I have developed still more friends. In fact, the campout and the backpack trip have begun to function as a central activity for developing friendships. Each year there are new faces, new friends, and new experiences. Interestingly, some nonalcoholics join us from time to time. During the AA meetings we have during our outings, they marvel at the intimacy and level of honesty they hear in our discussions, which we in AA take for granted.

By simply following commonsense suggestions, my life has changed in ways I never could have predicted or produced on my own. Through Steps Four and Five, I recognized what I lacked and by applying corrective action, especially with Steps Six and Seven, my life has changed immeasurably. Willingness to accept the reasonable advice of another, and an honest effort to put it into my life were key.

I entered AA as a lonely, wretched, ignorant, and isolated practicing drunk, and I've found exactly what I always wanted—to be a part of something wonderful, and to be valued by others who are also a part of it. It's what I was looking for all along. My experience is exactly what I think is described as God doing for me what I could not do for myself.

T. T.

Albuquerque, New Mexico

Best Friends

Grapevine Online Exclusive - December 2011

I am a Black woman from Texas, whose spiritual path could be described as "New Age." Maria is a Puerto Rican who was raised in New York City and is a devout Catholic. I have less than two years continuous sobriety, and Maria has more than two decades. By some quirk of cosmic synchronicity, we have become best friends.

I stormed into the meeting room of my home group on December 7, 2009, full of anger at myself that I had yet again disappointed everyone. At the suggestion of a friend, I had placed myself on a waiting list for a treatment facility. Being on that list had made me awfully thirsty, and still thinking my addiction problems were with "outside issues," I had gone to a bar on December 5 with every intention to have just two drinks. Needless to say, after that first drink, the insanity hit me and the party was on. That was my last drunk. Two days later, I still desperately wanted to drink, and my anger was the only thing that was keeping me sober. That evening, I finally admitted to myself that I was indeed powerless over alcohol. A few days later, I went to the treatment center, determined to learn all they had to teach me.

Although I had visited AA briefly many years earlier to get some papers signed, I hadn't had any interest in listening to anything anyone had to say or in getting to know any of the people. This time, I listened to everything they had to say. I got a sponsor the day before I went to treatment, and we started working the Steps when I got out of the treatment facility. One of the things I heard in the rooms of AA was that it was usually a good idea to get a good friend in addition to a sponsor, because saying goodbye to the old people, places and things can leave a huge hole in our lives. I've never been a people person unless I was out drinking, but for the sake of my sobriety, I decided to give this friend idea a try.

First, I tried to cultivate a best friend relationship with a woman I met in treatment. She was as serious about recovery as I was and we relied on each other a lot in the treatment facility, but when we got out, I went back to my apartment and she went to one of the local extended-stay missions on the other side of town and found other friends. I felt left out.

Although the women in my home group were kind to me, I still felt a little like an outsider. Most of them had known each other for years, and I was the new kid on the block. There were other women in my home group who were a couple of months ahead of me, but they were either young enough to be my daughters or were married with children. There were other newcomers, but most of them either didn't seem very serious about the program, or I didn't feel a connection with them. Since I've always been a loner at heart, I gave up on the best friend idea.

When I was about two and a half months sober, my sponsor suggested that I attend a local womens' group in addition to my regular home group. Several women in my home group attended this particular womens' group, and I rode with one of them to a meeting. In addition to women from my home group, there were women from other groups, and also women who considered this to be their home group. I enjoyed the meeting and vowed to become a regular attendee. The next week, the woman who had given me the ride the week before wasn't going to be able to pick me up, so she called another woman to substitute. Maria showed up on my doorstep, and I rode to the meeting with her.

Although Maria had a couple of decades in the program, she had only been in the area for a few months, and was building a local support base. She tried to organize a "Sober Womens' Movie Group," and for a while, four or five women would attend movies together, then it whittled down to just the two of us. Maria and I are both single with no children, and most of the other women had families. It was easy for us to be spontaneous. From movies we branched out to restaurants, art galleries, the theater, shopping, parties, and holiday celebrations. Sometimes we'd meet over coffee or ice cream because one of us needed to talk.

When I was about four months sober, and still a little nervous about going places where alcohol was served, I won two tickets to the theater, so I invited Maria. The usher looked at our tickets, and gave us directions to our seats, "... walk past the bar, and turn right." We both laughed. I made it to my seat without getting jittery.

Friday nights used to be my big drinking nights, so when I got sober I was apprehensive about going to restaurants on Friday evenings. Restaurants are packed with people and tend to be noisy on Fridays, and most of them serve alcohol, so although I love dining out, my solution on Fridays was to sit at home nursing a big piece of chocolate cake. Maria is at a point in her sobriety where noisy restaurants don't bother her, and thanks to going out to dinner with Maria, noisy restaurants don't bother me as much anymore either.

It's good to have a best friend, and it is one of the things that has helped to keep me sober. I have grown in my recovery because of my friendship with Maria, and I'm glad that our Higher Powers put us together.

Sheila R.

Fort Worth, Texas

Real Friends

Grapevine Online Exclusive - May 2011

How often have you heard a newcomer share at a meeting that since he joined AA, most of his old friends have stopped coming around and that he thinks that he is losing them? Sometimes this may be distressful and may cause a person to question whether the sacrifice is worth it.

Sometimes the word "friend" is misunderstood. We often refer to the people we are associated with as friends. Some will say that you can count on one hand the true friends you will have in a lifetime. So where do these associates/acquaintances come in?

I played golf for about 35 years and had many so-called "golfing friends," but when the round of golf was over, we put our clubs in the car and went our separate ways. Fishing was the same. When we finished fishing, we put our rod and tackle box in the car and went home.

With these acquaintances, the common denominator was the golf or the fishing. That's what bound us to each other. I quit playing golf about five years ago and now that the common denominator is gone, I seldom see my old golfing friends except in passing, where we exchange pleasantries and again are on our ways.

Most of the friends I had before I was sober had only one thing in common with me and that was the drinking. Unlike the golf and the fishing, we could drink 24 hours a day if we wanted to. We didn't need a boat or even a set of clubs to associate with each other. A bottle was all that was necessary, and without it we had very little in common. When the common denominator was gone, trying to hang out with them became awkward for them and for me. I had to accept that reality and let them be. If we have anything else in common we will know it and share that association with each other, but that was seldom the case, except for family members or work associates.

We in AA are fortunate indeed, for we have a common denominator that has been likened to survivors of a sinking ship in a life boat. We associate at such a deep and intimate level that we develop true friendships that the average person seldom is exposed to. Understanding this can be a great comfort to that new member who has to be prepared to move on.

Rick R.
Poway, California

CHAPTER SIX

Pets and Animals

Sometimes victims of our addiction, they become one of recovery's rewards

"My dog was as close as I unwittingly allowed God to get," writes S.K. in the story "A Canine Step Nine." When members can finally look honestly at their active pasts, there's often an animal in the wreckage, suffering along with family, friends and cohorts. These are poignant, powerful stories of how, once sober, we learn to show up for our four-legged friends and become open to the things they can teach us.

In "Ala-Cat," a cat shares identical physical symptoms with its owner, C.B. A furry creature brings a message from Pat S.'s daughter in spirit, in "A Fox in the Woods." In the story "Puppy Love," as Paul F. reaches seven months sober, a dog named Alex proves that Paul can do more than shuffle from meeting to meeting, and even that he is indeed ready to become a parent. "I learned to express joy, to persevere even when it seemed impossible and, most important, I learned to laugh," Paul writes in tribute to his sobriety and his Alex.

Like our humans, our animals need to be reassured that things have changed, one day at a time. In the story "Jake," writer M.S. says to her anxious cat as she leaves for her meetings, "You're lucky, kid. I've got the program!"

A Canine Step Nine
March 2013

When I was in the grips of my alcoholism, my dog was as close as I unwittingly allowed God to get. I loved and trusted my pet a whole lot more than people, especially those who had my best interest at heart. In retrospect, I discovered that my expectations of people were quite disproportionate to reality. Nevertheless, my dog would lie patiently by my side while I nursed yet another "justified" resentment wrapped in a hangover. And she would lie there all day, if necessary. Even some days in sobriety now, when I'm tempted to withdraw from the human race, my dog keeps me tethered to life. Thank God for my dog.

As I make another inventory at this five-year mark of my recovery, I reflect on the place my dogs have had in my life and the amends I owe them. Some may balk ... making amends to a dog? Well, hear me out.

During my active alcoholic years, I must acknowledge my dogs' inconsistent and unacceptable treatment by me: Staying out late, not coming home at all, irrational fits of yelling which left them running for cover, feeding them cheap food, forgetting to feed them at all, no real exercise, minimal play time, little attention, and intolerance for accidents on the carpet, which were really my fault. With each selfish, irresponsible decision, I piled up more and more guilt and shame, which I doused with a drink. So, making amends to my pets makes perfect sense to this recovering alcoholic.

Today, I make my K-9 amends much like I make my living amends to my human family. I begin by asking my Higher Power to keep me sober each day and walking in the sunlight of the spirit. And every day, I do the one thing that God cannot do for me, and that is to surrender my will to something much bigger and better than me. I follow this up with lots of scratches behind the ears, milk bones and plenty of love and ball fetching. I never had any children. Like many alcoholics, my pets are my family. I look at the relationship between me and my dogs as a commitment—and a gift of grace from God.

A beautiful quality about dogs is one they share with God—forgiveness. One of life's highest pleasures is being enthusiastically greeted at the door by my devoted and trusting dog.

S. K.

Alma, Arkansas

Ala-Cat

September 1983

My cat was a blue-point Siamese, and if there were an Al-Anon for family pets, she would have been permanent chairman!

When she was young, she was long, lean, affectionate, active, and intelligent. She was also spoiled, demanding, vain, and very concerned with her own appearance and comfort. She alternated between elaborate independence and plaintive bids for approval and reassurance. Her flights of evasive stubbornness and disobedience were always followed by highly vocal, loving requests to be petted. In a social "people group," she gravitated toward the men, talked a lot, ate the crabmeat off the canapes, and even though she didn't drink the cocktails, turned delighted somersaults in the center of the room to get attention. Sound like someone you know?

This cat was acting like an alcoholic, a reflection of me while I was breezing along socially but drawing closer to the brink of the abysmal alcoholic addiction into which I was ultimately to fall. For 10 years, she lived alone with me and shared it all.

When I became a solitary, at-home drinker and didn't eat, the one thing I did was for her—crawling downstairs to feed her. She shared my bed (of alternating agony and oblivion), lying pressed against my legs, staring at me with a look I shall never forget. Sympathy? Admonishment? Puzzlement? Sometimes, she sat up on the bureau in that characteristic haughty, noble pose of the Siamese cat. When I awoke and hallucinated, I saw only that image of her all over the room, papered on the walls and ceiling, printed on the curtains and bedspread. I never could figure out which in that myriad of cats was really she.

I suffered broken bones from falling down the stairs or onto the floor. On waking, I often had to look around to see what room I was in, wondering how I got there. The cat was always beside me, waiting, talking, licking my face. I did a lot of screaming, crying, swearing and praying; at those times, she stayed at a frightened distance but never dropped that steady gaze.

Everything was confided to her, all the mad, lonely, paranoid feelings. The ringing phone and doorbell were ignored, and she came to understand that I couldn't have made it to answer either one. Holding her tightly, I told her she was my only friend (by that time, I had very few) and told her we didn't need anyone else. She would wail and cry along with me, sharing my self-pity. But gradually, she would become annoyed with it all and angrily dive in, bite me, and depart to wander through the house howling, taking her frustration out by eating voraciously and drinking endless bowls of water. She became disobedient and didn't quite trust me.

Today, in sobriety, I can see how she reacted like a member of the family—with sympathy, pity, disdain, and anger, voicing her helplessness at this beloved creature who kept changing daily and whose behavior she could no longer understand. After 16 weeks of hospital, rehabilitation, and the AA program, I had learned about the "family disease" and Al-Anon. That cat had become as sick as I. When I came home after treatment, I was eyed suspiciously from a distance for a few hours. After she was convinced that I was somehow different and safe, she leaped into my lap, chattering loudly to be petted, and contentedly fell asleep there.

Our relationship was much like the early days when I was raising her from a kitten. She became more devoted than ever, and I can still say that she was my best friend, whom I loved more than any other.

The animal psychologists claim that family pets often take on the mannerisms and personality of the owner or whoever feeds, loves, and trains them. My veterinarian says that the pet and the person also undergo a neurotic and physical interchange of illnesses with identical symptoms. He observes this often in his practice and pointed out such a pair that had been in the waiting room with me.

Unfortunately, in her last three years—sober, happy ones—while we were growing old together (she was past 100 in cat chronology), we both developed physical problems: progressive bone disease and kidney failure. Once again, we shared the same symptoms, suffered the same pain.

My present husband and my married daughter began to attend Al-Anon when I was first hospitalized with addiction to drugs and alcohol. We are now a loving, understanding family, but the cat is no longer with us. How she helped me to realize what they had endured!

I prayed a lot during her illness, preparing myself and gaining strength to face the euthanasia that was inevitable, and I have never lost a loved one for whom I shed as many tears. I do know that AA, Al-Anon, and sobriety helped me to grieve my way through that great loss. Very gradually came a new attitude toward death, an awareness that grief was good and cleansing for the soul, an absence of fear, an acceptance of God's will—all things that I had never before experienced.

God bless my Al-Anon cat. I'm sure he has.

C. B.

Hershey, Pennsylvania

Puppy Love
February 2003

O ne of the greatest gifts of my sobriety has been the ability to do things I could never have done as a practicing alcoholic. I've just returned from my veterinarian's office where my whole family gathered to put our dog, Alex, to sleep. For anyone with a pet, this kind of death is traumatic. As a recovering alcoholic, there's more to it for me than that. Nearly 13 years ago, Alex became the first demonstration in my life of the Twelfth Step, that we practice these principles in all our affairs.

Alex was the answer to the question: Would I ever be able to do more than shuffle from meeting to meeting and puzzle out this blueprint for living within the rooms of AA? Neither my wife nor I were looking for a dog when Alex, a stray, came to us. We were barely beginning to wonder, bleary-eyed, who we had married back in the throes of our addictions. I was seven months sober, and Alex was the first real change I made in my newfound life after alcohol. The routine of feeding, walking, and caring for another living being was the first baby-step toward outward change that I was able to take. From the beginning, Alex was a symbol of my strengthening recovery and the presence of a loving Higher Power in my life.

For years, my wife and I joked to our AA and Al-Anon friends that Alex was proof that we could be good to any children that God chose to place in our care. For the first decade of sobriety, when our Higher Power said "not yet" again and again to children, Alex was our child. As he grew older, caring for him taught me many lessons that later proved so beneficial when God finally did bless us with two beautiful daughters.

I learned the importance of constancy, of companionship, of love that demands no return. I learned to express joy, to persevere even when it seemed impossible, and most important, I learned to laugh. As a practicing alcoholic, I missed the opportunity to experience the good and bad that life had to offer in so many relationships of much greater importance before Alex arrived. Alex taught me how to live those emotions in a caring, productive, and nurturing relationship that allowed me to try on my new sober principles before I was put to the test with a crying newborn or a questioning two-year-old.

I can't tell you how many times in the rooms I've heard the drunkalog about kicking the cat or abusing the dog and thought to myself, Thank you, God, that I did not do that. Or how many times I heard the same drunkalog about a damaged child and said to myself, Thank you, God, that caring for Alex taught me I do not have to do that.

In his last few years, Alex grew old and frail. He climbed stairs slowly and with pain. His eyes were those of the old: gray and opaque. He heard and saw less. An inevitable end, one I likely would have missed or failed to fully experience if I were still drinking, lay clearly ahead. This, too, was one of the gifts of sobriety. After years of joy and love, my wife and I had to make the painful decision that our beautiful dog's quality of life was so poor that death was a better choice. Alex's death reinforced for me so many of the principles of this program that govern my life today.

Today, as an alcoholic who not only doesn't drink anymore, but depends upon a Higher Power and Alcoholics Anonymous for guidance, I can make the most difficult decisions. Today, as an alcoholic who strives to practice these principles outside the rooms as well as in, I can be there for my family in a difficult time. Today, as an alcoholic who can actually think about people other than himself, I can make the healthy choice to gently and lovingly introduce my two young daughters to one of the most important and defining events in life: death.

And today, in remembering my beloved Alex, I can try, as he did, even on his last morning, to live as we all hope we can—one day at a time, with a focus on the moment at hand, with no regret of the past or any wish to shut the door on it.

Paul F.
Wexford, Pennsylvania

Jake

February 1984

n June 1978, two months after my first anniversary in AA, I found a kitten, and I knew in the instant I picked him up that I had been given a reward and a responsibility. Today, he is a comfort and a joy, and I tell about him whenever I qualify.

When I was in the deepest shadows of drinking and incapable of taking care of a beloved cat, he died. Our beautiful Butternut was one of the victims of our alcoholism. With his death, the last link of communication between my husband and me was severed. We grieved for him, but we grieved separately. Five months later, my husband was dead in a nearby park, and I was alone—but about to be rescued.

I was taken to a hospital where I was nurtured, where I learned again how to take a shower and wash my hair, how to eat with a knife and fork, how to sit in a chair and not always on the edge of a bed. I learned something about alcoholism and began to learn about myself. I was given clothes and medicine, food and books, and finally was given just the tiniest glimmer of hope. One night, I heard myself laugh, and that gave me more hope.

After I was discharged, I went to AA meetings and began making phone calls and then friends. I thought that someday, maybe, I could be happy. I thought many times of getting a kitten, and I talked a lot about the possibility of having one, and I talked and I talked and I did nothing.

Two months after my first anniversary, on a sparkling June morning, I found him, my Jake. I was on my way to work, and he was sitting in the middle of the sidewalk. I looked down, and he looked up, and it was decided. I picked him up, and he began to purr—this wee furry tiger, this stray, this abandoned alley-cat baby. He trusted me, and I knew that I could take care of him, that I was going to be given this chance, this gift, because I was sober and he needed me—*me*, not just anyone who happened along. I carried him home in the palm of my hand and left him with a saucer of milk and went to work.

He was waiting when I came home. I was determined that he would not be neurotic, as our other cats had been, as I had been. I found him on a Wednesday, bought him a carrying case on Friday, took him to the vet Saturday morning for a checkup and shots, and threw a party for him that night. There were 10 recovering alcoholics and one small cat who greeted everyone, who enjoyed himself immensely, who still enjoys having company, listening to conversations, and butting in whenever he can.

It had been over 15 years since I'd had a kitten, and I'd never raised one alone. Jake taught me patience and tolerance and how to laugh at myself, and he helped me relax. He is a reward and a responsibility. It's comforting to know that he's never smelled alcohol on my breath or my clothes or my skin, never seen me stagger or lurch or pass out.

Like all cats, he puts on a sad face when I leave him, but like all cats, he doesn't really mind being alone. I was hesitant in those early days but couldn't skip any meetings. So each time I went out, I'd lean down and say, "You're lucky, kid, I've got the program!"

I know it's more than luck. I know it's God's blessing. But it's a ritual that pleases us both.

M. S.
New York, New York

A Fox in the Woods
October 2001

W hen I tried to apply the Steps of AA to my grief over the death of my 30-year-old daughter, Phyllis, I came to a brick wall. I could admit I was powerless over death. No amount of prayer, bargaining, you-name-it had stopped the inexorable progress of the ovarian cancer that invaded her body, despite surgical intervention and chemotherapy.

Phyllis had attended a spiritual retreat when she was in her early 20s. She told of having something unresolved since the death of her father when she was 16, and she had taken a walk in the woods during the retreat to meditate on this issue. When she had finished her meditation, she asked her Higher Power to give her some sign that her prayer had been heard. As she continued to walk, a fox stepped out of the woods onto the path ahead of her. She stopped walking and watched the fox, who looked at her for a long moment, trotted up the path a few feet, then turned and disappeared into the woods after a backward glance at her.

A few weeks before Phyllis died, her husband was reading to her about the fox from a book on animals and their significance to Native Americans. The book mentioned that the fox is believed by some to be the bearer of messages to and from the spirit world. This was of tremendous significance to Phyllis inasmuch as it confirmed to her that the fox she had seen at the retreat had, indeed, been the sign that her prayer had been heard.

A few months after Phyllis's death, I visited a place near our home where there are rapids along a creek that I frequent when I want to talk to God (I feel less self-conscious talking out loud with the babble of water over the rocks). That day I had something exciting to tell Phyllis. After I had finished, I started to walk away when I added, as an afterthought, "If you heard me, would you please let me see a fox on my way home?" I started up the path toward home, looking left and right to see if there was a fox on one side or the other of the creek, and ahead to see if there was one on the path, but there were no foxes.

Then, just as I was about to turn away from the creek and start up the hill to our house, I glanced to my left one last time and my eyes fell on a sand bar along the creek. There, to my amazement, was a young fox playing with a stick, tossing it up and pouncing on it like a puppy with a toy. He did this several times as I watched, sinking to my knees to thank my Higher Power for this gift.

I go to the rapids often to talk to God and to Phyllis. I don't have to ask for a fox; I know they hear me.

It has been almost five years since Phyllis died. I still miss her and have days when the pain of grief is as fresh as when it was new. These are the days when I am reminded to be grateful that I have a Higher Power to turn to and a program from which to derive the strength to get through another day sober, in spite of my powerlessness over life and death.

Pat S.

Newark, Delaware

For the Love of Ruby
March 2002

Five months of sobriety should have made life easier to cope with, but instead, each day became a tougher battle to fight. I'd never been a social drinker and I was even less social as a sober person. The thought of venturing out into the world without something to steady my nerves was almost incomprehensible. I'd become a prisoner of fear in my own small apartment. My treatment center counselor, my fellow AAs, and my family all gave suggestions designed to get me out of my apartment and into the world. None were in the least bit appealing until someone suggested I get a dog. Now that hit a chord.

I have loved dogs all my life and had two until I graduated from high school. I had planned on getting a puppy as soon as I graduated college and was settled down somewhere. That never happened. Life and my alcoholism had other plans. My first job out of college had me traveling most of the time. Getting a dog would have been impossible. Soon, my drinking took over and I found myself bouncing from job to job and state to state every few years.

I finally landed in treatment in early 1990. I'd only lived in Denver a few months and knew no one except for the few people I worked with. Without a bottle to give me courage and keep me company, I was bitterly lonely, and the outside world became unbearably frightening. I masked my fear in anger and the two emotions came very close to destroying me. I'd force myself to go to meetings but the minute someone approached me, I'd duck out of the room. If I had no escape, I'd be very cold, answering questions with one-word answers, hoping these AAs would leave me alone. I didn't know what to talk about; I felt awkward and inadequate and was uncomfortable with even the slightest bit of attention.

It was obvious to everyone but me that I needed to learn how to live outside of my own head. I needed a distraction, I needed something that I could take care of and be responsible for. I needed something or someone I could be responsible to. I needed love and, most of all, I needed a Higher Power.

Then, a coworker showed up at work one day chattering about a new litter of pups that her Labrador retriever had just given birth to. I tried to shut her out because I was living in an apartment that didn't allow dogs. I thought I was doing a pretty good job of resisting until the day she brought in pictures. She told me that all the pups were scheduled to be adopted except one. It was a runt, as she called it, and she said that it would probably end up at the shelter. My heart broke. I knew what it felt like to be cast aside because you were less than perfect, and I wanted to cry when I thought about that little dog.

I asked her if I could come by after work to take a look at the last pup. She agreed and an hour later I walked out with that little bundle in my arms. I wasn't sure how I was going to hide a Lab in my apartment, but when that little black pup looked up at me with eyes that said, "Please love me," I knew I would find a way—and I did. I named her Ruby.

I scraped together as much money as I could and put a down payment on a small house with a large backyard—plenty of room for Ruby and me. Behind the house was a large expanse of undeveloped land—acres and acres for us to run free. Suddenly I had something I had to be responsible for and responsible to. Granted, a dog wouldn't call me on my stuff or give positive feedback when I read my Fourth Step, but Ruby was a start.

I began walking her every day, which is how I got to know all my neighbors, something I would have never attempted alone. I took Ruby to AA meetings with me. I even took her to work sometimes. She gave me a reason to step outside of myself, a way to forget my problems, a reason to take care of myself. Ruby took the edge off my fear and gave me a starting point, a comfortable level for me to begin my recovery.

My world began to revolve around Ruby. In a sense, she was my first version of a Higher Power. Somehow, she knew when I was struggling and seemed able to reach out and touch my very soul. Whenever I thought about giving up, all I had to do was look into her eyes and suddenly, no matter how bad I felt, I knew I had to get through it for her sake; I couldn't bear the thought of letting her down. She was depending on me to stay strong.

Somehow Ruby taught me how to love myself. Maybe because she always loved me even when I didn't want her to or maybe it was because she still loved me when I felt as if I was unlovable. All I know is that there were times that I hung on for no other reason than for the love of Ruby.

The lessons of love that she taught me gave me the strength to move back to my home state of Texas and face the ghosts I'd been running from for so long. Here, I have built a new relationship with my family, gotten married, and have a life today that I only dreamt of before. I am sure that I couldn't have stayed sober without the love that little black pup taught me. With the courage she gave me, I've been able to start my life over with hope for the future.

I've been sober for 11 years now, and Ruby has been gone for a year. I wasn't sure how I would handle it when she passed. I had depended so much on her for strength, and I worried that the floor would collapse beneath me when she was no longer here. That didn't happen. My loving husband, my new family, and my faith carried me through.

What I learned was that it was God all along who had been keeping me sober. In the early years of my sobriety, I was too self-centered and too cynical to believe in most things that I *could* see—I wasn't about to turn my will and my life over to the power of something I *couldn't* see. God, in his infinite wisdom, understood that the best way to communicate his message to me was in a form I would love and would be able to understand: a dog.

Stacy M.
Azle, Texas

A Friendly Dog Story
July 2003

During my last years of drinking, I developed many phobias, and some of these irrational fears persisted well into my sobriety.

One in particular was my fear of dogs. I do a lot of walking for exercise, and for a long time, whenever I heard a dog barking I would immediately change course. During one period in my life, I walked to my favorite restaurant for lunch every day, about a mile away. I did not take the most direct route after finding out that there was a big dog at a house along the way. The dog was not tied up. My fear and avoidance of dogs was really bothering me, and finally I decided to use Steps Six and Seven on this fear. I said my prayers and proceeded to walk past the house with the dog. As I went by, I waved and said a friendly "Hi" to the dog. The dog barked but did not chase me.

For a number of days, I continued giving my friendly greeting, and the dog barked as I went by until one day, it did not bark; it just looked at me. More days passed with the dog no longer barking, and I continued my friendly greeting. Then one day as I was passing by, the dog walked up to me and let me pet it. This was a spiritual experience for me, an awareness of God working in my life as the dog and I became friends. In the days that followed, even though the dog did not come up to me again, I felt its friendliness whenever I passed by. It was as if we understood and accepted each other.

Joe R.

Indianapolis, Indiana

Tiger in the Tank
April 2009

God told me to talk about a kitten at an AA meeting. I was married to an active alcoholic. When I first got sober, I criticized her drinking and nagged her to attend AA meetings. That strategy failed miserably, and we both ended up drunk.

Recently, I got sober again. This time I have not pressured my wife. I have shown her the same compassion that other AAs have always shown me. One morning I took her truck to a garage for repairs. The owner arrived a few minutes later. He opened his car hood and heard a gentle mewing sound. A terrified kitten trembled next to the radiator. She had ridden in the engine compartment for 50 miles, remaining miraculously unhurt. I volunteered to bring her home.

The garage owner asked me to name her after the make of his car.

A week later at my AA meeting I was celebrating 60 days of sobriety. I was going to speak and I prayed for guidance. A tiny, gentle "God" voice in my head said, "Tell the story about the kitten." I argued that it had nothing to do with alcoholism. "Just tell it anyway," the voice replied. So I told the story about the kitten in the engine and then thanked the group for its support in my early sobriety. No one complained.

A few weeks passed and my wife took the kitten to the vet for a checkup. The kitten has long black fur and gleaming yellow eyes, and everyone in the waiting room made a fuss over her. My wife carried her in, greeted the vet, and introduced the kitten by name. "Is this the kitten that was found in a car?" asked the vet.

My wife was stunned. "How could you possibly know that?" she asked. "I attended an AA meeting the day your husband collected his 60-day chip and shared the story of the kitten," the vet responded.

"I think I have a problem with drinking," my wife whispered. The vet spoke very tactfully about AA. She did not say one word about my wife getting sober. She simply described her life as a drunk and how much better life had become since she found AA.

My wife returned from the vet's office and said, "I'm going to get sober." And that's why God told me to talk about a kitten at an AA meeting.

John W.
Conifer, Colorado

CHAPTER SEVEN

Sponsorship

Experience, guidance, love and sobriety are the gifts of this special one-on-one bond

" saw firsthand how an adult could be man enough to say honestly, 'Ouch, I'm hurting,'" says the author of "Sponsor Relationships," the first story in this section on sponsorship. E.S. now had a clear mirror image of a man much like himself, but sober. A grownup. His sponsor.

Each of these revealing stories offers another facet of AA's unique, two-way practice that enriches the sobriety of sponsor as well as sponsee. In "90 Days of June," Carol P. admits her program was lacking depth. At 27 years of sobriety, her gift of desperation was the humility to finally ask for help.

Sponsorship often works in surprising and delightful ways. In "Quiet Guidance," a sponsor's advice is given to the story's author "with a strange little smile I didn't understand for years ... Thelma did not tell me to grow up. She allowed me to grow up."

In the story "An Unfamiliar Bond," Steve, a perfectionist with "a resentment-choked idea of God," shares his Fifth Step with a sponsor "that opened up things I had welded shut behind steel doors," things he did not even want to write down, freeing him forever. After finishing his Fifth Step, Steve was sure his sponsor would call the cops, curse him, or at least throw him out. "But instead," he writes, "he served me chili."

Sponsor Relationships
September 1975 *[Excerpt]*

One sponsor plus one group equals sobriety! That's what was suggested to me in my first week. However, I often saw some other newcomer claim four or five groups as home groups, pick a liberal, a moderate, and a conservative as sponsors, ask all three for advice, then do as he pleased. And he stayed sober! Which is the better way? As the Siamese monarch said in "The King and I," "It's a puzzlement."

I can laugh and joke with a changing crowd, but I need a familiar few to hurt and cry with. I did a lot of hurting the first couple of years. The first sponsor I had picked me. He swooped down on me and said, "Stick around, kid. You're in the right place." He had me making coffee and driving the gang to a speaking commitment in Connecticut in my first month. Connecticut! I hadn't gotten out of Brooklyn in 10 years. I bragged about it as if I'd been invited to the French Riviera. At that stage, I needed someone to think for me, and my first sponsor did.

A whole series of other wonderful AAs befriended me along the way. Some had even less sobriety than I had. That was OK by me. If the Higher Power gave me answers through a newer person, I accepted them.

In my AA travels, I picked up a confidant who was particularly loving and kind. He was a tall, gangling guy, always in casual clothes, with a twinkle in his eyes and 22 years on me. He was a grandfather, with a lot of common sense. I met his mother, sisters, and grandchildren. We went to beach parties and movies together and played golf.

Tom was the greatest teacher I ever had. Do you want to know one of his greatest teaching tools? He shared. It was that simple. Tom not only shared his family and life and joys, but privileged me by sharing his troubles as well. I saw firsthand how an adult could be man enough to say honestly, "Ouch! I'm hurting!" In the process, I learned how to confide, use the telephone, and relish the Fifth Step.

Tom knew as much about me as I knew about myself—or probably even more than I could bear to admit about myself at the time. He once pinned me to the wall by saying, "Ed, you have an absolute genius for talking *around* a problem. Some day, you'll get honest and call a spade a spade." Eventually, I did. He was a gentle man and allowed me to grow up in my own time. He was great with tender egos, patient beyond belief.

One day I went up to him and said, "Tom, I never asked anyone to be my sponsor. You're it—OK?" I felt foolish. He beamed his best smile and said, "Uh, sure, Ed. We'll work it one day at a time. But tell me—what do you think it is we've been doing for the last 18 months?"

Tom died suddenly one day. Sober. I knew his view of death, so I was not unnerved. To him, death was just another state of being. He had helped me overcome my gnawing fear that everything ended when we died. You see, he had not just backslapped me and sent me on my way—he had shared in the fullest sense of the word.

That kind of sharing usually is a once-in-a-lifetime thing. If you have it more than once, you are fortunate beyond belief. For a spell, I floated in the program without a sponsor. I had never really liked the word, anyway. Because of my ego, "sponsor" sounded ominous. I heard sober people use other words, like "coach," and didn't care much for them, either. But I also kept hearing speakers at meetings talk lovingly about their sponsors of 20 or 25 years ago.

Today, I have another close AA friend, a man who is in the same profession I am, has been sober a little longer, and has great balance in his way of life. I have filled him in on my past. I want someone who knows me near at hand. I want to be able to call any time and say, "Hey, Jerry, here's my problem." I'd rather not have to fill out a questionnaire first. I want Jerry to be able to give me advice based on what he knows about me—the whole story, not meaningless patches with meaningful gaps in between. Believe me, it took guts for me to fill Jerry in on "the great I," but it was good for me. It helped keep my ego in line. For me, this is an essential effort that must be made continually.

It is obvious that the word "sponsor" has a very special meaning (or meanings) to me. It changes as I change. My first sponsor helped me over the bumps. I needed a friend then very much. Later might have been too late. I am glad he didn't wait until *I* picked *him*. Then I needed a guide—Tom—who would let me find myself as painlessly as possible. Now I need someone—Jerry—to keep my Tenth Step inventory in order. I have always found the right person when I needed him most.

I have spoken to several people who think the patterns of sponsorship are changing in general. They claim that some new people are leery of commitment to a sponsor, just as some older members are leery of commitment to a newcomer. Fear of commitment can take exasperating turns. Here's what happened to a newcomer I know. His sponsor said he was busy, but would meet the newcomer any time he called. So the newcomer did call one day and was told to give more notice. On the next call, the newcomer asked to see the sponsor 14 days later. The older man said that he followed the AA program and could not project that far in the future! Sounds silly, but it happened.

Some AAs get shy about sponsoring people in and out of hospitals, especially at large detoxification centers. One or two abrupt rejections from a patient leave them doubtful about doing this type of Twelfth Step work ever again. I think we must remember that we carry the message and not the drunk. When a person is hospitalized, it's a golden opportunity for us, and we should not stop trying. No matter how outside circumstances change, most AAs feel that the new person still needs a friend in the beginning and that the older member still needs the spiritual experience of watching a new person get sober and grow.

My own experience as a sponsor has varied. I held on to one guy too long. I never will make that mistake again. A wise man said a sponsor should, just for a time, do things for a new person that he can't do for himself—and then turn him over to the conscience of the group. Sounds to me like a fine way to avoid any fears that either side may have of being possessive or being possessed.

And I've had the opposite experience—being asked to sponsor, then never seeing that newcomer again. I think some people ask me just because they think they should have an official sponsor, but rarely do they need me.

Still, there are people out there whom I have helped, I believe. I advised them to lean on AA, since that's what I lean on for independence and a fear-free life. These are my happiest sponsor relationships. There are many other AAs whom I share with. They don't call me sponsor, but they work out problems with me, and I do the same with them. I am not good as an authority figure who has all the answers. I am just fine as a sober drunk not too proud to admit I had a lousy night last night.

Now that I've reflected on sponsorship and its changing nature, I do not feel it is such a puzzlement after all. Each AA, as newcomer or as sponsor, must find the right method for himself or for herself. For this AA, the right formula remains: One sponsor plus one group equals sobriety.

E. S.

New York, New York

---

90 Days of June

February 2015

Ninety days ago, I asked June B. to be my sponsor. This was not an impulsive decision, by any means. But as I look back over the progress I've made this summer, I now wish I'd done this years before.

What brought me to finding a sponsor was that I'd hit an emotional bottom and was on my knees. I knew that something had to change, and that something was me. My plan was simple—get a sponsor. Beyond that, I didn't have a clue. I felt like a newbie. I had time in the

program, but I didn't have much depth. For many years, my AA trans-
mission had been firmly stuck in one gear: Step One. Now, desperation
drove my willingness.

But whom should I ask to be my sponsor? As my 27th anniversary
approached, I talked with June in the parking lot after a meeting. I
told her a bit about myself and about how I typically celebrated my
anniversaries in a private way—no spotlight, no fanfare. She suggested
that I get a chip presented to me at every meeting that I attended during that anniversary week. I initially balked, as I dreaded public speaking. But if I decided to ask June to be my sponsor, what tone would
it set if I refused to take her very first suggestion? Shaking with fear,
I stood up twice that week. Almost immediately, I felt a new sense of
belonging to AA, like I was finally a part of the program.

A week after my anniversary, I attended a Big Book Step Four workshop in Nashua, New Hampshire. Here I learned that earning money
is not my primary job in life. Money just pays the bills. The Third Step
says that we have a new employer who will provide for us if we "keep
close and perform his work well." This caused a shift in my perspective.
Just what was my role here on Earth?

After the workshop ended, I caught a glimpse of June and hustled
to catch up with her. Somewhere in that short sprint, I found the courage to ask her to be my sponsor. She agreed and gave me homework.
She told me that I had a message to share, although I couldn't see it.
Ten days later, I ratted out my disease by telling her that I had been
asked to go on a commitment and that I had declined. Clearly, "no"
was the wrong answer. I went on that commitment and told my story
from the podium. My fear of public speaking had prevented me from
sharing anything about myself. In discussion meetings, I used to say,
all in one breath, "Hi, I'm Carol. I'm an alcoholic." No wonder no one
knew who I was! In these past 90 days, I've spoken at four commitments. I learned that when I'm asked to help, I should say yes. And I
learned that I could survive public speaking.

June taught me the difference between good pain and bad pain.
Bad pain is a stabbing pain and requires professional attention. Good

pain just makes you uncomfortable, although it can be downright awful. I also learned, through many tearful phone calls, that I don't have to feel good to do good. One day June had me laughing and crying at the same time. No small feat. The tears indicated that something deep inside me had been jostled. Now, instead of being afraid of crying, the tears are a welcome flag telling me, "There's something important here—pay attention."

Before this summer, I had complete faith that the program worked for other people, but I had no faith that I had a personal HP. While I'm still trying to develop a relationship with a God of my understanding, I now have faith that the process can work for me too.

June taught me about "God pops." It is only when my brain is quiet and still, that directions from my HP can get through to me. June also assigned me 90 meetings in 90 days. And it wasn't to be just any 90 meetings. I was to select seven meetings and to stick to that schedule for 13 weeks. First, I learned humility: a 90 in 90 isn't just for folks fresh out of rehab.

While I resisted this assignment (to put it mildly), it was a wonderful way for me to step out of the shadows completely. Week after week people saw me and learned my name, and I learned theirs. Having a specific meeting to attend each day grounded me. I planned my day around the meeting, not the other way around. This in turn taught me about priorities: AA comes first. It also taught me about committing to a task, arriving on time and staying for the whole meeting. Now I go even when I'm not feeling well, or when I simply don't want to go.

June stipulated that I was to raise my hand high at discussion meetings and share. I had rarely raised my hand (or been at the podium) in 27 years, so this was very uncomfortable territory for me. June reminded me that doing what was comfortable clearly hadn't worked for me, as it had eventually driven me to my knees, so the way to grow was to do the "opposite of feeling comfortable."

If the meeting format precluded me from sharing, then I was to call three people in the program and ask them how their day was going. Only one problem—I hated the phone! After June saw that I was eventually comfortable calling people who I knew well, the assignment was modified to calling three strangers. "Pick up a phone list at all of your meetings, and use it," she told me. June frequently uses role-playing as a way to teach, so we had a few practice conversations. This taught me how to reach out to a stranger. Some of these strangers are now good friends. It also dawned on me that someday I might be on the receiving end of a stranger's call.

By calling June every day at a designated time, I learned about structuring my day. When my morning call was getting later and later, I readjusted after a simple reminder. I learned that I have to resist making up my own rules; by doing so, it shows that I can take directions.

Over the course of these 90 days, a few people have commented on the positive changes that they see in me. And best of all, I also see the good changes within me. I am happier. I am kinder to strangers. My boiling anger has cooled to a simmer. I'm seeking a personal God in my life. I can meditate for more than five minutes now. Tears are no longer shunned. For a long time, I was out of sight of the herd, and now I've been accepted into the fold. All this in 90 days, all because I was willing to reach out for help to a sponsor—who, in turn, guides me toward God's open arms.

Carol P.
Clinton, Massachusetts

Dumped
February 2012

was sort of new to the area and had established myself as a regular at a few meetings, but I really didn't "hang out" with anyone in the program because I had a pretty full social life already, between the constant companionship of my husband and the busy lives of my children, grandchildren, sisters and friends outside AA. So it kind of surprised me when a newcomer asked me to be her sponsor. I had always thought sponsors were supposed to be part of the "in" crowd, visible members of AA, people who are known to be good sponsors—not little old stand-offish me.

Anyway, I said yes. I was thrilled to be asked, and it helped that I really liked this newcomer and wanted to do a good job helping her. And, over the next year or so, I think I did do a good job. I was there for the late-night crying spells, and the family drama stories, and the good things too. We read the Big Book, worked the Steps, and when the time was right, I encouraged her to sponsor others and to take on commitments.

After a year of hard work, we were moving into cruise control and she was doing well, weathering storms with her new set of AA tools, helping others and getting rid of a lot of excess baggage and old drama. I had begun to hear from her less and less and found myself calling or texting her to ask her how she was doing. She was beginning to ignore me. One day I got an email saying, "Thank you so much, blah blah blah, I think I don't need to have you as my sponsor anymore." Ouch! Hello! Hello? What the h—!

Being fired in an email. How embarrassing! I wanted to bury my head (and then send her an email that would make her do something different than what she obviously wanted to do). But I did nothing in that regard. I sat with it, stewed over it, wrote a thousand snarky emails in my head. And then of course I called my sponsor. I expected her to listen sympathetically and say, "You did a good job, now do a Fourth Step on it." Instead, she said, "Oh yeah, that happened to me when I was having my kidney disease and was in the hospital every other week and my sponsee fired me because I wasn't there for her. Now she's the secretary at my favorite meeting, and I get to see her every week, and she totally ignores me. Never asks me about my kidney transplant or anything." Well, that certainly topped my tale of woe. At least in the case of my sponsee, she had done me the favor of disappearing entirely off the local radar, so I didn't have to be reminded every week that she dumped me.

OK, so my conversation with my sponsor gave me some perspective. Also, she finished by asking me some key questions, such as: Did my sponsee recently get a new boyfriend? (Yes.) "Hmmmm," she said. Then she related other stories of sponsees she had had who got new boyfriends and then dumped her, and she let me know that I was to pray about the situation and let it go.

So I did what she said. I did send one email response to my sponsee and told her that being dumped in an email took me by surprise—that it hurt my feelings and my ego. It was short and it was true. The truth is that the way she handled it was bad form. I'd like to think that one of the things I've learned in AA is to stay honest in my relationships and not to drop them as I was now being dropped. But I didn't say that, since I was no longer her sponsor—I had no more wisdom to impart. I simply kept my response to a few words, saying that I felt hurt by being dumped in an email. I give no excuses for my response.

Now for the happy ending. In the weeks following this blow (I call it that because that's how it felt), I had a number of feelings come up that I was not used to. Although I often got a resentful feeling in my gut, it usually passed very quickly. More importantly, I noticed I was feeling sadness—and hurt. I had lost a relationship that I had liked, and I had been hurt by someone I had loved. I was hurting inside, and that was a very unusual feeling for me. Remember, I have a loving husband and two great kids, some good close friends, a couple of excellent sisters and very dear grandchildren. But I was hurt and sad because someone I had cared for had not cared for me, or had not cared enough to continue our relationship.

What happened as a result of this was to me sort of a miracle. I suddenly found the need to start reaching out to other women in my life, to see how they were doing and to let them know how I was doing. I began to be more of a friend to those around me, especially the terrific women I knew in my AA groups. My loss had created a need in me to draw closer to others and to draw them closer to me. I realized for the first time how much I loved the women I had come to know in my new AA groups. It wasn't that I didn't love them before, but I loved them from afar. Now, for the first time, I actually needed them. And they were there. We began to call each other, to spend time together, sharing our experience, strength, hope, sadness and laughter. I had been too self-sufficient before. Now, thanks to my sponsee who broke my heart, my heart was broken open for others to come in. They say God never closes one door without opening another. I believe God used her to close one door so that another could open—the door of my heart.

The happy ending is that a couple of months later, when I was chairing a meeting on my 10th AA birthday, my old sponsee showed up and publicly thanked me for helping her. I still don't know if she ever understood how much I was hurt, but it didn't make any difference. Having had a spiritual awakening as the result of these Steps, through this experience with her, I had carried the message to other alcoholics and practiced the principles in all my affairs.

Anonymous

An Unfamiliar Bond
March 2008

Before I found AA, I tried everything—from years of counseling to support groups and self-help books. No matter what I did, my home, work, friendships, and spiritual life were a mess. Maintaining this mess required picking fights, showing off at work, defying rules, obsessing on being abused as a child and as a teen, throwing tantrums, panic attacks, screaming rages, brewing resentments, recurring bouts of depression, putting others down to prove I was right, self-injury, fear of people, temper tantrums, unrelenting perfectionism, fear of poverty, and getting fired often. Trying to hide the above and explaining to family and friends why I moved from job to job required increasing creativity.

For relief, and to forget this misery, I binge drank—always in secret.

This continued in irregular bouts for 20 years, marked by months— or even a year—of not getting drunk. At the start of a night's binge-ing, alcohol reliably dulled my pain. By night's end, drinking opened wide the spigots of self-pity and risky behavior. Rolling on the floor in drunken crying jags was a sure bet, as was suffering remorse and shame later over the stupid, risky things I did when drunk.

Hector, a binge beer-drinker I knew, was arrested, convicted, and "sentenced" to AA. Hector, too, had a rough childhood and a quiver full of resentments. After a while in AA, he changed. Hector stopped drinking, stopped stealing, made sober friends, and even camped and hunted with his "sponsor." It was amazing. Could AA help me?

My first attempt at finding a sponsor was a flop. After two months of attending from five to seven AA meetings a week (in another county so no one would recognize me), I had somehow stayed sober. I felt I didn't fit into AA—my problems were paltry compared to some in leads I heard. I had not so much as a DUI or a stretch in jail. A guy at a meet-ing told me that I needed a sponsor to understand AA. Being a per-fectionist, I was apprehensive about making the "wrong decision" on a sponsor. The guy suggested I look for a temporary sponsor as a start.

There was an influential guy, "Stan," who sponsored many at a meeting I attended. Stan talked freely of big-money deals, ran a large company, and hired many new, unemployed AAs—in other words, an ideal sponsor.

I asked Stan to be my temporary sponsor. He agreed to talk with me over coffee at a restaurant. Stan told me, "The only way you'll stay sober in this program is to be born again, accept Jesus Christ as your personal Lord and Savior, and join the Church." Stan was a pillar of a fundamentalist congregation that hosted AA meetings.

I was stunned. I harbored seething resentments against organized religion, and told Stan so. I'd used resentments and buckets of self-pity as excuses for binge drinking. I told Stan I'd get back to him and de-cided to go somewhere else—fast.

I began attending meetings in yet another county. There, I met Will, a man with 22 years' sobriety. He saw I was new and patiently answered my questions. In a bout of tears, I poured out my failure in seeking a temporary sponsor. Will said he came to AA with powerful resentment against formal religion. In AA, Will found a God of his own understanding, a "Higher Power." Will said I would, too, and that this Higher Power would help me stay sober. Will recommended a mens' meeting where I could ask the secretary to point out a temporary sponsor. In Will, I'd finally connected to someone like me.

At the mens' meeting, the secretary pointed out two temporary sponsors. The secretary knew most of the AAs in the room—those who followed through and those who were just "good talkers." That's when I met Mark and asked him to be my temporary sponsor. Mark promptly said, "Yes." Then he instructed me to read "The Doctor's Opinion" in the Big Book, phone him in two days to check on how I was doing, join him at a mens' discussion meeting, and discuss my homework with him afterward.

As I learned later, this was a test. Mark wanted to see (1) if I would follow through and (2) if I could follow directions. Most guys whom Mark had asked to do this didn't follow through. Mark, with 20 years of sobriety, met with me regularly thereafter by phone and in person, returning calls for help, assigning more to read in the Big Book, talking after meetings, and starting me working on Step One. Mark said he sponsored one or two men at once due to job and home commitments. He said I'd need some other AAs as co-sponsors to help. I suggested Will as a co-sponsor, and Mark said, "Ask him." Now, I count three kind, caring men with long sobriety as co-sponsors. Mark warned me if I spent too much time with these AAs, I'd end up being sober.

Mark worked slowly and patiently. He mercilessly pointed out my "drama," as he called it. Once he deflated the drama, he took on my need to have everyone in AA approve of me, an obsession to make friends I didn't know how to handle, picking and choosing rules I would or would not follow, being disrespectful toward others, identifying my role in creating a problem, and, finally, completely avoiding any situation or person who generated sizzling anger in me.

Mark persistently challenged my alcoholic thinking, pointing out distorted understandings of situations and people. He was quick to voice his sober view on most things—at length. He told me to stop comparing myself with leads as I "had gotten off the alcoholism elevator at a different place from them." He said I didn't have to go to the bottom of the elevator to be helped by AA. Though I had less time drinking and paid fewer consequences than some, my sponsor maintained that I had the same crazy thinking as any other alcoholic, and that this thinking, if not changed, would lead me to a certain and unhappy death.

Weeks passed, and I felt I didn't fit into my home group. At meetings, I sulked, arrived late, and stared at my feet. So Mark told me to clean the coffee pot after meetings. I did it once, and felt better. I had a purpose in the group. I stayed after every meeting and left the kitchen and our things clean. Eventually, the secretary asked me to buy candy for meetings. This increased my feeling of purpose, and the "candy-eaters" quickly learned my name.

Anger and fights at home were problems. Typically, I made my point in family fights by throwing and breaking things. This was preceded by poking at sore spots, dredging up old fights, and so on. Mark taught me that I was half of every fight, and I had to take a walk when a fight began or was about to ignite. If I threw or broke anything, I had to call Mark right away. He had me apologize immediately—"cleaning up my side of the street." Soon, the embarrassment of having to report throwing something to Mark curtailed most of my throwing matches. My sponsor helped me see I could actually control my fighting, first by a little, and later by more.

Mark taught me to pray. When he asked me to kneel at his side and say the Third Step Prayer with him, I freaked. All I could think of was running away. Though I had attended worship for decades, I had never actually prayed, much less while kneeling next to another man. Somehow, I squeezed by that Third Step prayer with my sponsor and then ran from his house.

A few weeks before, a moment of clarity arrived at a meeting. I was inspired to trash the entire, resentment-choked idea of God I dragged with me to AA. Suddenly, I felt free to choose a brand-new God of my own understanding. Over the next few weeks, my sponsor helped me sort out my Higher Power: AA, my home group, my sponsor, people who had cared for me, and things I found beautiful. This was a Higher Power I could live with, and I didn't have to drink over it.

Last month, Mark saw me through my Fourth Step. Undertaking this thorough and fearless moral inventory of my resentments, money problems, sexual problems, and fears caused many sleepless nights. I felt expected remorse for things I easily remembered and unexpected remorse for things I had pushed into the shadows. When done with my Fourth Step, I had both a desperate desire to get it off my chest and an equally strong desire to burn and scatter what I wrote. I, the master of my universe, was surprised to discover that fears drove my actions and ruled my life. Mark assured me it was the same for him. He told me that I was no different from others in AA whose unrecognized fears had orchestrated their lives.

Mark located an AA named Paul for my Fifth Step. I barely knew Paul, but I was told he had long sobriety and survived an abusive up-bringing like mine. I was terrified at the prospect of telling my most shameful transgressions and secret thoughts to a total stranger, but Mark told me to trust his word and trust my Higher Power that things would be OK. The way I was brought up, trust was both dangerous and foolish. But somehow, I had begun to trust Mark.

Completing my Fifth Step with Paul took two sessions. It generated overwhelming feelings of both self-loathing and relief—a strange mixture. The Fifth Step opened up things I had welded shut behind steel doors, things not written on my papers, things that pushed me to hate myself, to drink, and to forget. At Paul's encouragement, I spared nothing in my Fifth Step, and in doing so, I was spared. After finishing the Fifth Step, I was convinced Paul would curse me, phone the police, and throw me bodily from his house. But instead, he served me chili.

I needed a couple of weeks to calm down after my Fifth Step. During that time, I bonded with Paul, asking him about the strange feelings I was having, calling occasionally to add something I'd left out of my Fifth Step. But Paul assured me all was well. I stopped feeling self-conscious or ashamed in front of him. I began to feel a sort of kinship with others in my home group who had completed their Fifth Step.

I am nearly 11 months sober now, and Mark continues to chip away at my alcoholic thinking as we begin the next Step. He points out that I "melt down" only twice a week now, down from four to five times a week when I started. Recently, he insisted I shake hands with everyone in my home group before the meeting began. I refused, certain I would burst into flames if I did so. As a sober person, I find looking people in the eye and shaking their hands frightening. Not only will I see them, but they'll see me. And, though I was convinced I'd explode, my sponsor was right: I survived shaking hands. Now, I actually enjoy shaking hands. This is totally unlike me. I've begun to change.

Steve
Elyria, Ohio

Quiet Guidance
May 1990

Whenever I hear sponsors mentioned in AA meetings, I think about the sponsors I've had since September 1974, when I first got to AA.

I remember my first sponsor. Let's call her Wilma, since that wasn't her name. I asked her to be my sponsor after my first AA meeting. Wilma was the only one who spoke to me before the meeting, and she spoke with great enthusiasm about AA and sobriety for some time during the meeting. Someone had said during the meeting that having a sponsor was very important. So I quickly asked Wilma to be my sponsor. I also picked her because she made me feel comfortable. We were very much alike in personality and attitudes. She even thought it was hip, slick, and cool that I was gay, even though she was definitely heterosexual.

But I stayed sober only about 90 days. I went to lots of AA meetings and had great enthusiasm about sobriety, but I don't remember working any Steps. I got drunk shortly before Christmas 1974. But about nine months of drinking was all I could take before crawling to the phone to send up a white flag of surrender. I still vividly remember the phone call I made to Wilma that September day when my ego had been squashed like a bug on a windshield and I was desperate to get back to AA.

But Wilma was drunk. She'd started drinking a few weeks after I did. After I found my own way back to AA, several people told me that Wilma had been in AA for a number of years but had never been able to stay sober for more than about a year.

I waited almost six months this time before getting serious about picking another sponsor. And I read the Big Book and began working the Steps.

About the time I saw Step Four looming on the horizon—working the first three Steps daily had become automatic—I started searching for a sponsor. I talked after meetings and over coffee with some of the older members of the groups I was attending, and I still believe they gave me some good suggestions on how to go about finding a sponsor.

One fellow told me to only consider those who'd been sober for at least seven to eight years. This, he felt, was long enough for them to get over what he considered to be the silly and egotistical habit of summarizing their sobriety as a set of rigid rules which they then foisted upon their sponsees.

"Remember," he said (in so many words), "thousands of drunks all over the world have gotten and stayed sober solely on the basis of the AA program as described in the AA books and discussed in meetings. But all you know about one person's special rules is that one person has stayed sober by following them."

Another person told me to watch out for people who reminded me too much of myself in terms of personality, attitudes, or outlook on life, because, if we were very much alike, we'd share the same blind spots.

A third person suggested I consider someone who had something that I wanted for myself in my future sobriety—not someone who had what I already had.

And someone else told me to check people out. "See if they walk like they talk," she said. "Check them out with some of the old-timers so you don't pick someone who's making habitual use of AA's swinging door," she added, knowing my earlier experience with Wilma.

Another woman in AA gave me some specifics. "When you find someone you think might fill the bill," she said, "get a phone number and use it. Do this with several people. Use them as if they were your sponsors by calling them when you have a problem or a question. Do this for a while and you'll find yourself eventually calling only the person who'll be a good sponsor for you. The others will drop by the wayside. They won't be home most of the time when you call, or they'll be too busy to talk to you when they are home. They'll want to do all the talking and won't be able to listen to you. Or you'll be afraid to talk to them about problems for some reason you may not be aware of until you try. The important thing," she continued, "is that you'll end up with the right person this way, even though you're not doing the picking. It'll feel to you like your sponsor is picking you. It's like what they say about coincidences being the way God works best, and that God does his best work anonymously. Your sponsor will be picked for you in a way that seems like a coincidence, but it won't be," she said with a strange little smile that I didn't understand for years.

I followed many of these suggestions, the most difficult being to ask people for phone numbers and then call them. But I made myself do it, for the person who'd suggested I try potential sponsors out on the phone for a while had also said that if I couldn't do this now, I might not be able to do it later.

When I was about nine months sober, I picked as a sponsor a woman I never would have picked when I was newer. Thelma was very much unlike me. I was in my late 20s; Thelma was about 60. I was definitely a lesbian; she was definitely not. I was a university graduate student; Thelma had made it through high school. She even wore all those bright and ill-fitting house dresses—clothes I would never be caught dead wearing.

I could tell right away that she wasn't bigoted against gays, for when I mentioned I was homosexual, she didn't bat an eye. She just looked at me as if I'd confessed to liking popcorn. And the look said better than any words can that my sexual orientation had nothing to do with AA, sobriety, or her as my sponsor. In this and other ways, Thelma made me feel at home in AA, and I lost that feeling of being different. After a few months of having Thelma as my sponsor, I even lost the feeling I'd had most of my life that if people *really* knew me and all that I'd done in my life, they'd tell me to get lost. I became just another alcoholic in a room full of alcoholics.

I remember what Thelma told me when I asked her to be my sponsor. She told me that she could be my sponsor as long as I remembered one important thing: She had clay feet. "Don't put me on a pedestal," she said. "If you do, I'll fall off."

Thelma had nothing especially new or insightful to say on how to stay sober or work the Steps. On sobriety, she said, "To stay sober, don't drink." Whenever I asked her about working the Steps, she just said, "Read the book. The directions are in it."

Thelma was definitely spiritual, the quality that had drawn me to her in the first place. But there wasn't a religious bone in her body. This proved fortunate for me, for I did not know it then but the sober years to come would show me I had some deep-rooted resentments against organized religion based on childhood experiences, including a parent's use of God as a punishing and vengeful deity.

It has taken years for these wounds to heal. During that time, all I could do to help the process was choose not to practice, a day at a time, the resentments that had grown like scabs on these childhood memories. This especially meant not getting caught up in similar resentments expressed by others in meetings.

Thelma told me about the Great Spirit of the universe, since she was half American Indian and found the Indian practices and beliefs more in keeping with her own spiritual experiences. She never lectured me about spirituality, but then Thelma never lectured me about anything.

Thelma always listened to me, no matter how long I needed to talk. If I was ranting on about some injustice I'd experienced, Thelma let me rattle on until I ran out of steam. Then she would tell me about an experience she'd had when she was certain that someone was treating her unjustly. The endings of such stories drawn from her experiences were always the same: "And then time passed, I got over my hurt, and later found out I had been wrong about that person." She'd find out that the person she'd thought was intentionally hurting her was doing no such thing or that the injustice she'd felt was no injustice after all.

I must have done a lot of ranting in those days, for I can remember hearing about a number of Thelma's experiences of this sort. At other times, when I had no problems and we were just talking, Thelma would patiently tell me about how impossible it was to know the truth when anger locked me into my own point of view. But she usually phrased it as the need for "walking a few miles in the other person's moccasins."

In meetings, those who didn't know her probably thought of her as a quiet older woman who sat in the corner and listened carefully to everyone who spoke. From her example, reinforced by others I knew in those days, I learned how to quiet my mind and truly listen to others so that I could hear what I needed to hear that day.

One old-timer explained it this way to me: "Don't let your mind rattle on at meetings. Then all you'll hear from someone else is something that gets you thinking about what you have to say. Listen to everything the person talking has to say, as if your life depended on it—because it might one day. Listen to everyone this way, especially the ones you want to ignore," this old-timer said. "God won't deprive you of the answer you need, if you've come to an AA meeting needing an answer. He may, however, have your answer come out of the mouth of the person you least expect to have your answer. God has a sense of humor."

I never heard Thelma criticizing anyone other than herself. If she didn't agree with someone, she was silent or spoke about something else. And when I asked her a question, Thelma wasn't afraid to say, "I don't know. Let's ask someone else."

The most consistent policy in Thelma's approach to sponsorship was her refusal to give me advice about anything. If I phoned her about a problem, she would listen carefully, not interrupting even if I took five minutes to give every insignificant detail. After a moment of silence, Thelma would share with me one of her experiences. Sometimes the experiences weren't similar, but the feelings or reactions were the same. Thelma never used sharing experience as a roundabout way of telling me what to do, either.

In talking about her experiences, she was vague about the details but very clear about her feelings and even clearer about what she had to consider before making a decision. She was much clearer about the process of making that decision than she was about exactly what decision she made.

It took me years to realize what Thelma was doing—not only teaching me how to make decisions on my own but also how to see the common thread running through human experiences so I could avoid getting sidetracked so easily by the details.

Once she said something like this: "If I told you what to do, and it worked, you would have no one to thank but me. All you would learn to do is be dependent on me to do your thinking and deciding for you. Even though you want very much right now for me to tell you what to do, if I did this you would one day come to hate me for it, because one day you would resent it as a way I have kept you weak and powerless."

Thelma told me that, no matter how much I feared making bad decisions, I could not learn how to make good decisions except by making decisions. "You'll make mistakes," she said, "We all do. You will make some bad decisions before you learn how to make good ones. But what is true about good decisions is also true about bad ones: You will always learn from the consequences."

Thelma did not tell me to grow up. She allowed me to grow up. She gave me lots of elbow room for growing, giving me no rules to follow (or break) regarding meetings to attend or required check-in phone calls or visits to her. As I grew, I began to learn as much from her methods as from what she said to me, especially in the years that followed when circumstances took me hundreds and then thousands of miles from Thelma.

Thelma was my sponsor. She was never my Higher Power. I say was because Thelma has disappeared from the face of the earth. Some call this death. But what is important is that I haven't lost Thelma. I've just gained another invisible means of support.

Anonymous

The Choice
June 1991

Step Six: Were entirely ready to have God remove all these defects of character.

All of them? As Bill W. points out in the chapter on Step Six in the "Twelve and Twelve": "Some people, of course, may conclude that they are indeed ready to have all these defects taken from them. But even these people, if they construct a list of still milder defects, will be obliged to admit that they prefer to hang on to some of them."

Several years ago I had a vivid personal example of what he was talking about. At that time I had a sponsor to whom I was devoted, one reason for which, possibly, was that she and I shared some of the same characteristics or, as some would say, defects. One of them was a quick temper. Restraint of tongue and pen didn't come easily to either of us.

One day, after a brisk altercation on the phone, she hung up on me. Indignation swelled up inside me. That was absolutely no way for a sponsor of many years' sobriety to behave! Indignation was followed by a delicious sense of grievance, of having been profoundly wronged.

For the next 24 hours I fed and watered that delightful sense of victimhood. I would not, of course, have admitted for one moment to myself or anyone else how much I was enjoying it, or my discovery that being a victim was not far removed from (in the words of the Prince of Denmark) a consummation devoutly to be wished. In my own mind I replayed the incident on the phone over and over, brushing aside my recollection of what I might have said or done to bring on my sponsor's action. And each time her hanging up on me grew more heinous. I was innocent, and in a case like this, innocence is power.

The next afternoon, after being out of my apartment for several hours, I called my answering service to pick up messages. The young woman at the other end of the phone said, "Jean called to say she's sorry and would you please call her."

You would think, wouldn't you, that now, with my sense of grievance fully vindicated, I would be filled with joy and forgiveness? You would be wrong. My first feeling, and I remember it well, was dismay, followed quickly by a flattening sense of letdown.

I worried at that letdown for a full day before some glimmering of its real cause dawned on me: I knew that when I would call Jean she'd repeat her apology and I would have to forgive her. And by forgiving her, I would yield up the sense of power, of self-justification, that I had enjoyed so much.

It took me another several hours to define what my choice was: I could have my grievance or I could have my friend. Not both. I had to choose. And I saw further that choice is one of the fruits of sobriety that by putting down the bottle I now had, not only about this, but about other aspects of my life and other defects of character. It was the first time I understood a defect for what it was: something out of which I derived pleasure or power and was therefore not entirely willing to give up. Obviously, in this particular example, by relinquishing the pleasure I would get something better—the restoration of friendship.

But sometimes the sense of gratification, of power that a grievance can bring, is hard to yield up. I once heard a well-known doctor, one of the first to recognize what AA could do, say, "Self-pity is followed by isolation is followed by a drink."

And I began, especially after the incident involving my sponsor, to understand why, when I first came into Alcoholics Anonymous, the most frequent warnings from some of the old-timers were against self-pity. All those sensations I'd been wallowing in with such enjoyment—of being aggrieved, of being wronged, of (for once!) being in the right, of being victimized—added up to the heady brew of self-pity. And I then comprehended fully why self-pity, leading to isolation (and wasn't I isolating myself from my sponsor?), was presented by that doctor and the old-timers as such a formidable enemy of sobriety.

P.S. I called Jean and we made up and the incident passed. But I still think about it a lot.

Isabelle H.
New York, New York

... And Learn
November 1996

am always quick to acknowledge the contributions my sponsors have made to my sobriety, but I often forget the growth I've attained from the ladies I sponsor.

I became a sponsor for the first time when I was 11 months sober. I'd never read the pamphlet on sponsorship so when Tina would call with overwhelming newcomer problems, I'd pick her up, bring her to my house, tuck her into bed with a stuffed animal, and say, "We just won't drink tonight and tomorrow everything will get better." Somehow it always did and eight years later Tina is a sober mother and almost finished with nursing school. I wasn't so lucky with Beverly. After release from a mental hospital, she checked into a hotel with a bottle of pills and a quart of vodka. I learned that I have no answers, only experience. If I haven't lived it or done it, I need to send the newcomer to someone who has.

Jackie taught me to live and let live. She gave me the courage to leave my grown children so we all might make our own decisions and lead our own lives. Five years later, we are all doing well and one daughter has joined Al-Anon.

I'd never been to a prom so being Kim's bridesmaid and wearing a formal filled that void. Later I was allowed to witness the miracle of her daughter's birth. Phyllis taught me about kindness, and Sheila taught me to be a friend. Shirley taught me to never give up, Rose taught forgiveness, and Vickie taught trust.

I came to AA looking for a way to drink like a lady. What I found was hope and self-respect, unconditional love mixed with honesty, tolerance, and understanding. By working with others I'm allowed to witness the miracle of sobriety and observe the twinkling eyes as others learn to speak the language of the heart. Like me they came to scoff and stayed to pray. I thank God for lessons learned and pray that I'll never be too old or too rigid to learn from everyone in the Fellowship of Alcoholics Anonymous.

Eileen K.
Orange, California

Sweet Goodbye at the Farm
January 2013

I don't do death," I once said to someone in the rooms, just being a smarty. The truth is, I had always been away when important people in my life passed away. They all died suddenly and so I was shocked, saddened and mostly relieved that they hadn't lingered, and that I didn't have to watch them suffer. I would always just arrive in time for the funerals.

Then Jamie came into the rooms and changed all that. She was about 33 years old and dying of cancer when she asked me to be her sponsor. She looked healthy at the time, had a great sense of humor, and had a wild multi-colored hairdo (she was in show business). In fact, she had left her rock band on tour in Europe to come home to her sister's farm outside of Baltimore, because she was no longer in remission.

When she could not attend meetings anymore, we brought the meetings to her. I can still see that handful of AA women sitting outside her home with her because the weather was still nice. The meetings were not about dying, but about living—sober.

One day, we were all complaining about our jobs, relationships— you know, all the usual stuff. When it was Jamie's turn, she let out a sigh, lifted her face to the sun, and said, "Ah, luxurious problems." She was so relieved not to be in pain (she had decided not to take any pain medication), and very grateful to be sitting in the sun with her friends.

"Ah, luxurious problems." I have never forgotten those wonderful words, especially when I am fussing about the stock market, car trouble, or not having "enough time."

Finally the day came when I got that much-dreaded call from Jamie. She said, "They tell me I'm dying. Will you come?" I replied that I was on my way.

"Dear God," I prayed, "you know I don't do death. Help me please to do and say the right thing." I shouldn't have worried because as soon as I walked into Jamie's room she asked me to pray with her. She then asked me to go for a walk with her boyfriend, who had left the band in Europe and flown back home to be with her. "He's in the program, and I want to make sure he'll be OK."

So, he and I walked this wonderful farmland road together and talked AA. I had the good sense to say little and let him share about Jamie. I remember our conversation like it was yesterday, even though it was a good 16 years ago.

When we got back from the walk, the family was there, and I made my exit soon after that, but not before saying the Release Prayer with

Jamie: "I love you and I release you and I let you go. I let you go to your good. The good of one is the good of all. I pray you get everything you want, and more."

On my ride home, I thanked God for the honor of being able to be there with her. I couldn't shake Jamie's concerns for her boyfriend and hoped when my last days came I would be thinking of someone else.

Jamie died the next day. The funeral was at the farm. It was everything I'd want mine to be and more. We all told stories of our time with Jamie; then a video of one of her performances was shown. Oh my God, there she was: what energy, what beauty, what a voice. And I had no idea.

Now, when someone is complaining about their sweet, sober life, I'll look up and say, "Ah, luxurious problems."

Mary Carol R.
Baltimore, Maryland

A Kid Like Me
March 2009

My first sponsee was a young man barely 17 years old. He attended the daily after-work meeting of my home group. He seemed a nice enough kid. But from his overall appearance and attitude, in addition to the fact that he was already in AA at such a tender age, it was evident that he had a pretty troubled past.

When he asked me to be his sponsor following one evening's meeting, my mind instantly swirled down the checklist of self-doubt that so many drunks seem to carry in their heads. The question that loomed largest was this: What does a 40-something-year-old have to say to a 17-year-old that could possibly make any sense?

Although I had no good answers, I said yes. My young friend had found lots of trouble in his short life. He was a prisoner in our state's juvenile justice system, sent to a state facility in our city 90 miles away from his hometown. That dug up a mean and ugly goblin from my past that I had hoped would stay buried forever.

Some 15 years before, I had spent a short, stressful and thoroughly disillusioning time working in what used to be called a "reform school" in another state. I was just out of college and looking for work, when a friend working as a counselor at the institution recommended I take a look at an exciting possibility. It was the 1970s and reform of juvenile justice systems was sweeping across the nation. My friend's institution was looking for young, bright and energetic people to transform its mission. I signed on. But just four months and three positions at the facility later—my last job was night watchman at one of its dormitories—I quit; exhausted, my ego crushed and absolutely convinced that kids in these places were beyond redemption.

Now, like Banquo's ghost in "Macbeth," this troubled teen appeared, bringing with him reminders of the resentment and self-loathing of my own dismal failures. But I had learned enough by that time to know that being willing is the key to all things in AA. So we talked. I kept any mention of my own experience in juvenile justice to myself, feeling this could only complicate matters for both of us. And, surprisingly, we got along fine, so much so that I actually looked forward to our half-hour talks once a week after meetings.

A couple of months of this went by and Thanksgiving was approaching. My sponsee was being sent back to his hometown for the holiday, his first visit in more than a year and a half. The trip would be more than a vacation, however. It would be a test to see if he was ready to go home for good, which could come in time for Christmas.

Sitting down for our last talk before his journey, my young friend was unusually surly. He told me he knew he would be seeing old friends and would be in old places, and he was afraid he was going to dive back into old behavior. We talked for some time. However, my advice, encouragement and assurances were met repeatedly with, "Yeah, but ..." Suddenly, those old memories I had kept hidden burst to mind, and I realized this kid was talking just like the boys I had heard so often 15 years before.

So I decided to tell him my story right there. I told him that he and I both knew that boys who end up as wards in "the system" have to screw up pretty big and pretty often. I told him that we both knew that the reason why this is so is because nobody could make people like him do anything they didn't want to do. Their parents couldn't make them go to school. Their teachers couldn't make them work when they got there. The cops couldn't make them stay out of trouble. And even punishment couldn't convince them not to do it again. I concluded: "So don't tell me that anybody can make you drink or drug if you really don't want to."

There was a long silence as he just sullenly stared at me. Then he broke into laughter. "You're right about that," he said.

I saw him the Monday after the holiday, and things had gone fine. Two weeks later, he was headed home for good.

My rather stern lecture to my young friend had deflated my shame about that painful episode in my life. The terrible memory that I ran away from had been transformed. Being willing to share my experience, strength and hope with another alcoholic enabled me to put an old goblin to rest once and for all.

Pinky G.
Skaneateles, New York

Words of Love
June 1991

"You're not going to like what I am going to tell you." How I hated those words that I heard for the first time one evening when I called my sponsor to talk to her about all the things that were going wrong in my life. She listened very patiently, without saying a word, while I spilled my tale of woe to her.

When I finished talking, I was sure she was going to agree with me that things were not going right for me. Instead, there was a silence on the other end of the phone for a few minutes, then she spoke those words: "You're not going to like what I am going to tell you." She was right, I didn't like what she said, but she was right in what she did say to me.

She told me that I was feeling sorry for myself and that I ought to get out of myself. She told it like it was. She said that I had no monopoly on pain or suffering or problems and that there were other alcoholics who had far more suffering, pain, and problems than I had and instead of making a self-pity list of all the things wrong in my life I ought to make a gratitude list of all the things right in my life.

She reminded me that this program does not guarantee me freedom from the problems of life, but it did guarantee me a way to live and deal with the problems. She also reminded me of the Third Step and to let God do his job. She said that I could not change the past or control the future, but I could make the most of living in today. She reminded me of my gift of sobriety and my freedom from the life of hell I lived in before.

I didn't like it when she suggested that I might be indulging in self-pity, a very dangerous indulgence for an alcoholic. But as she spoke to me I began to realize that I was heading in the wrong direction and she was guiding me back to the right way of thinking. My sponsor told me what I needed to hear, not what I wanted to hear.

That night her tough, loving words guided me from being a self-pitying, resentful martyr to becoming a grateful recovering alcoholic. Now, when I talk to my sponsor and I hear her say, "You're not going to like what I am going to say," I listen because I know they are words spoken with love and words that I will grow from.

I know it is not easy for her to say this at times when she knows I am hurting, but I am grateful that she refuses to let me slip into the trap of self-pity.

June W.

St. Louis, Missouri

Under the Renoir
February 2015

When I was new in sobriety, I met a woman who did not offer the kind of enormous affection I always craved. But she had everything else I wanted. She had a mansion on the water, with an art studio, a yacht, a handsome husband, 10 children, and an art gallery on Main Street. She also had 10 years of sobriety and was at meetings all the time doing needlepoint.

I was willing to do everything to get what she had—except the needlepoint. For a long time she said she didn't know if we had a generation gap or if I had brain damage. She kept telling me, "Walk like you take up space; don't walk like you're invisible!" I detoxed in the rooms and was pretty far gone in my mind. It took many grownups and prayers to bring me back to life.

When I told this woman all my secrets, all the things I had never told a soul on the planet, the resentments, guilt, shames and fears, she listened intently for six hours. I couldn't comprehend the Big Book or the Fifth Step, so she told me to just write my life story. When I finished reading it to her, she only said one thing, "You're a garden variety alcoholic." My isolation was over forever; I belonged someplace, I had been claimed out of the lost and found.

When I got hit by a car and was incapacitated for 14 months, she would have me come over to rest in the chaise lounge in her backyard, in front of the yacht. I would sip soda out of her silver Tiffany goblets, which her daddy gave her as part of her inheritance. I was on welfare, getting myself through college at the time, yet she treated me like a princess. She never once offered me money, and I never once asked for it. In time, I paid welfare back every dime.

When I earned a scholarship to paint in Paris, she threw me a go-ing-away party in that backyard, and I felt like I was Audrey Hepburn. I was living in a dream and couldn't believe I actually got to do my life over. I was fearful of leaving my boyfriend, my meetings, my life and going to France, but she would have none of that nonsense—I was going. That trip changed the entire direction of my life. Sitting at the American Cathedral at meetings every night was extraordinary. I wore the little quilted jacket she loaned me for the whole trip.

When I came home and started to date my husband, she said, "You don't have to do a Fifth Step with everyone you go out with! Our stories disclose in a general way what it used to be like." She got me on the road to normal. She moved away and I moved away, but we stayed in touch. My husband and I visited her in Key West when our twins were 2 years old. I remember changing diapers under the Renoir on her wall and thinking how far I had come because of her devotion to our program.

Over the years I'd visit her in Key West, and she was always thrilled to see me and I her. When she had financial problems, she told me, "You must paint. When I go to sleep at night, I don't think about the problems, I think about the colors." When her health be-gan to fail, she told me not to come and visit until she felt better so she could enjoy our time together. I happened to be in town and was determined to see her. I had a newcomer fresh out of detox in tow and went up to her apartment. I found out that hospice had been called. I parked the shaking girl on the couch right outside her bedroom, and the circle of our lives was right there on either side of the wall. AA teaches you how to live and teaches you how to die. We had our last conversation. She still couldn't understand why people thought she was so special and made such a fuss over her, because in her view she was just a garden variety alcoholic. Her humility, grace and gratitude were apparent at 45 years of sobriety.

Several weeks later, I got the call that she had passed. With that same newcomer in tow, I got a hotel room and went to the best funeral I've ever attended. At her art gallery people were eating and drinking, looking at all the beautiful photos of her life and her artwork and giving condolences to her family. Then at her request, we paraded down the main street behind a Junkanoo band, which led us right to the pier where she painted so many vibrant watercolors. We boarded catamarans and her ashes were scattered in the water—along with my Fifth Step. People surrounded us in other boats with her name written on their sails. She passed this way but once, and Alcoholics Anonymous made it count.

That woman was the most important woman in my life: she wasn't my mother, sister, cousin or friend—she was my sponsor. One of the definitions of holy is "spiritual respect." Holy is what we do for each other. We change each other's perceptions of ourselves, of the world and God. We bless each other with a sharing of grace like none other. We are in the miracle club, and our sponsors hold our hands and take us home.

Snow P.
Lake Worth, Florida

THE TWELVE STEPS

1. We admitted we were powerless over alcohol—that our lives had become unmanageable.
2. Came to believe that a Power greater than ourselves could restore us to sanity.
3. Made a decision to turn our will and our lives over to the care of God *as we understood Him.*
4. Made a searching and fearless moral inventory of ourselves.
5. Admitted to God, to ourselves, and to another human being the exact nature of our wrongs.
6. Were entirely ready to have God remove all these defects of character.
7. Humbly asked Him to remove our shortcomings.
8. Made a list of all persons we had harmed, and became willing to make amends to them all.
9. Made direct amends to such people wherever possible, except when to do so would injure them or others.
10. Continued to take personal inventory and when we were wrong promptly admitted it.
11. Sought through prayer and meditation to improve our conscious contact with God *as we understood Him,* praying only for knowledge of His will for us and the power to carry that out.
12. Having had a spiritual awakening as the result of these steps, we tried to carry this message to alcoholics, and to practice these principles in all our affairs.

THE TWELVE TRADITIONS

1. Our common welfare should come first; personal recovery depends upon A.A. unity.
2. For our group purpose there is but one ultimate authority—a loving God as He may express Himself in our group conscience. Our leaders are but trusted servants; they do not govern.
3. The only requirement for A.A. membership is a desire to stop drinking.
4. Each group should be autonomous except in matters affecting other groups or A.A. as a whole.
5. Each group has but one primary purpose—to carry its message to the alcoholic who still suffers.
6. An A.A. group ought never endorse, finance or lend the A.A. name to any related facility or outside enterprise, lest problems of money, property and prestige divert us from our primary purpose.
7. Every A.A. group ought to be fully self-supporting, declining outside contributions.
8. Alcoholics Anonymous should remain forever nonprofessional, but our service centers may employ special workers.
9. A.A., as such, ought never be organized; but we may create service boards or committees directly responsible to those they serve.
10. Alcoholics Anonymous has no opinion on outside issues; hence the A.A. name ought never be drawn into public controversy.
11. Our public relations policy is based on attraction rather than promotion; we need always maintain personal anonymity at the level of press, radio and films.
12. Anonymity is the spiritual foundation of all our traditions, ever reminding us to place principles before personalities.

Alcoholics Anonymous

AA's program of recovery is fully set forth in its basic text, *Alcoholics Anonymous* (commonly known as the Big Book), now in its Fourth Edition, as well as in *Twelve Steps and Twelve Traditions, Living Sober,* and other books. Information on AA can also be found on AA's website at WWW.AA.ORG, or by writing to:

Alcoholics Anonymous
Box 459
Grand Central Station
New York, NY 10163

For local resources, check your local telephone directory under "Alcoholics Anonymous." Four pamphlets, "This is A.A.," "Is A.A. For You?," "44 Questions," and "A Newcomer Asks" are also available from AA.

AA Grapevine

AA Grapevine is AA's international monthly journal, published continuously since its first issue in June 1944. The AA pamphlet on AA Grapevine describes its scope and purpose this way: "As an integral part of Alcoholics Anonymous since 1944, the Grapevine publishes articles that reflect the full diversity of experience and thought found within the A.A. Fellowship, as does La Viña, the bimonthly Spanish-language magazine, first published in 1996. No one viewpoint or philosophy dominates their pages, and in determining content, the editorial staff relies on the principles of the Twelve Traditions."

In addition to magazines, AA Grapevine, Inc. also produces an audio magazine, books, eBooks, audiobooks, and other items. It also offers a Grapevine Online subscription, which includes: eight to ten new stories monthly, AudioGrapevine (the audio version of the magazine), Grapevine Story Archive (the entire collection of Grapevine articles), and the current issue of Grapevine and La Viña in HTML format. For more information on AA Grapevine, or to subscribe to any of these, please visit the magazine's website at WWW.AAGRAPEVINE.ORG or write to:

AA Grapevine, Inc.
475 Riverside Drive
New York, NY 10115